A PRACTICAL CANADIAN MORTGAGE GUIDE

BY RICHARD STEACY

BOOKS BY RICHARD STEACY

Canadian Real Estate

Land Titles Registration in Canada and the U.S.A.
Published 1974

You Can Beat Inflation with Real Estate
Published 1975

Steacy's Practical Canadian Mortgage Guide
Published 1976

Listing and Selling Real Estate in Canada
Published 1977

A Practical Canadian Mortgage Guide
Published 1979
Revised edition published 1986

A PRACTICAL CANADIAN MORTGAGE GUIDE

BY RICHARD STEACY

Copyright © 1979, 1986 by Richard Steacy

Stoddart Publishing Co. Limited
34 Lesmill Road
Toronto, Canada
M3B 2T6

Published in 1979 by General Publishing Co. Limited
Second printing 1980
Third printing 1982
Revised edition 1986
First published in 1976 by Real Estate Press

*A mortgage guide cannot keep pace with the fluctuations
of interest rates. Rates used to help explain the way
money and mortgages work are examples only. Current
interest rates may be found in Chapter 31.*

Canadian Cataloguing in Publication Data

Steacy, Richard H., 1919-
  A Practical Canadian Mortgage Guide

ISBN 0-7737-5057-6

1. Mortgage loans—Canada—Handbooks, manuals,
etc. 2. Mortgages—Canada—Handbooks, manuals,
etc. I. Title.

HG2040.5.C2S73 332.7'2'0971 C79-094400-6

Typeset by Jay Tee Graphics Ltd.

Printed and bound in Canada

To my sons,
Charles Richard Graham Steacy
William Harold Denham Steacy
and their mother, Mary,
my wife

Happiness is being glad to get home . . .

Contents

Foreword

Where would we be without the mortgage? Living in cramped shacks, no doubt.

Who would have believed three or four decades ago that a labourer can today live in such luxurious surroundings, complete with broadloom?

Don't curse the mortgage lender. Bless him. He makes it all possible, and at a much cheaper rate than the loans on cars and a few thousand other items.

When we sign a mortgage deed, we borrow money. The rate of interest on this money is lower than money borrowed for other necessities (and luxuries) in life.

Who pays cash for a house? Usually someone who has just sold a house that was all paid for over a number of years. And how was this possible? By a mortgage or two of course.

I do not like a high rate of interest any more than you do, but when it comes to buying a home, it is a bargain.

To you who have built up your large equity in your home, remember that it was a mortgage lender who made it possible.

And to you who have yet to own a home, and want one, grit your teeth and prepare to sacrifice a bit like the rest of us. It will be worth it.

Borrower or lender, study this book carefully. It will surely improve your financial well-being.

Acknowledgements

I sincerely thank the following, and acknowledge their generous time and patience in helping with my research:

Robert Yeaman, a foremost Canadian specialist in the subject of interest rates and related mathematics, for his advice in preparing the chapter "Mortgage Repayment Schedules."

Mr. Robert Lajoie of Canada Mortgage and Housing Corporation, and Mr. Ryan of the Mortgage Insurance Company of Canada for their patience and good advice in updating much of my writing.

Richard Steacy

1
Defining a Mortgage

Who's Who

Mortgagee and mortgagor. You will find them throughout this book, also referred to as lender and borrower.

When you are a tenant in a building, you are a lessee. When you receive a gift, you are a donee. When you purchase goods, you are a vendee. Notice that each of the foregoing are ones upon whom a right is conferred. The right to occupy a building, the right to own the gift and the right to the goods purchased. Everyone on the receiving end is the one with the "ee" on the end of the name.

When one lends money to a real property owner, the property owner signs a mortgage deed and gives it to the lender. This is the lender's proof of security. The lender, receiving the mortgage from the borrower, is therefore the one to whom the right to the security is conferred. The mortgagee. The one with the "ee" on the end of its name.

Perhaps an easier way to remember who's who is to remember that the one with the "or" on the end of the name is the one who has title to something. The lessor owns the building which the lessee occupies. The donor owns the gift he is giving the donee. The vendor owns the goods he is selling the vendee.

And so it is with the borrower in a mortgage deed. He owns some real estate which he is using as a security for a loan, and is therefore the one who has title to something, the property.

The mortgagor. The one with the "or" at the end of the name. So the mortgag*or* (title holder) gives a mortgage to the mortgag*ee*.

Mortgagor	Borrower
Mortgagee	Lender

Defining a Mortgage

We all know what a mortgage is. Right? Wrong.

The noun "mortgage" comes from two French words, *mort* (dead) and *gage* (pledge). The pledge becomes dead when the loan is paid off or, as some say, the real estate pledged becomes dead (lost) due to failure to pay. Take your pick.

A mortgage is contained in a document called a deed. A mortgage deed is what we have. A deed is a document that contains a contract, or agreement, that is signed, sealed, contains proof of its delivery, and is effective on the date of delivery (to the lender).

It is signed by the borrower in English Common Law. In Quebec it is signed by both borrower and lender. It is often signed under seal. The seal is old hat; it signifies that the borrower was conscious of what he was doing when he signed the deed. So he signs it and sticks a seal on it.

The one signing places the seal with his signature. If one signed a deed and weren't conscious of the seal —in other words if the seal were placed on the deed after he signed and left the room—it wouldn't mean a thing. He must know about the seal at the time of signing.

You will find deeds in a land titles office with seals

and without seals. As a matter of fact some court judgements on the subject have said seals are unnecessary *period*, so if your lawyer tells you you don't need a seal, don't ask me to argue with him. But we must admit at least that a seal does make a deed look better.

Proof of delivery. Signing a deed in the presence of one's solicitor and giving the deed to the solicitor is considered to be proof of delivery, because solicitors act in trust. So the signing is trusting the solicitor to deliver the deed to the rightful party, and that's good enough.

It is effective on the date of delivery—which would be the date the signature goes on because that is done in the presence of a solicitor who is accepting delivery of it on that day for the lender.

There is a difference in Quebec and the rest of Canada in the handling of a mortgage deed and what it means.

In English Common Law (all of Canada except Quebec) there is, strictly speaking, only one legal mortgage. This may sound a bit confusing, but it is really very simple.

English common law says that the legal mortgagee is *entitled* to the *title* deed. There could be only one person *entitled* to the *title* deed in this statement, so he would obviously be the mortgagee who is the one who received the *first* mortgage deed signed by a borrower using the *title* deed as security. Once this mortgagee is entitled to the title deed by law, no one else could be entitled to it.

So a legal mortage in English Common Law is a first mortgage—but only a first mortgage registered against property in a *land registry office*. This requires a bit of further explanation.

There are two basic systems of land registration—

the registry and land titles offices. In land titles registration, the mortgage is a *charge* against the property, and therefore the legal mortgagee is not entitled to the title deed; he can't get it, because the mortgage is a charge on the property. Only in the registry office is he entitled to it.

Okay. So a legal mortgage in English Common Law is a mortgage of first priority in a land registry office. Well, what about all the other mortgages? Aren't they legal? Sure, but they are not called legal mortgages.

When one signs a first mortgage to be registered in a registry office, he is left with what is known as an equity of redemption. He has the right to redeem his property by paying off the mortgage. When one borrows additional funds, and signs another mortgage deed, he is borrowing against his equity in the property, and so this mortgage is called an equitable mortgage. So is a third and a fourth mortgage.

So a first mortgagee in a land registry office holds the (strictly speaking) legal mortgage, and the junior mortgagees in a land registry office hold equitable mortgages. But they are all legal. If it sounds like a lot of hocus pocus it is not intended to be, because apparently that is the way it is.

The legal mortgage is where we get the definition of a mortgage in that it is a conveyance of real property as security for a debt, and when the debt is repaid the property is returned, or reconveyed to the borrower. But not always.

You see, if there happens to be a second (equitable) mortgage registered against the property, the minute the first (legal) mortgage is paid off and discharged, the second mortgage automatically becomes the first (legal) mortgage.

Well, what about Quebec?

Now, here is a province that really knows how to define a mortgage. In Quebec a mortgage is called a deed of loan with hypothec. And get this—the Quebec Civil code goes on to define "hypothec" as being a "lien on an immovable" (which really is a first class definition of a mortgage without all the gobbledygook of English Common Law).

In Quebec no mortgagee is entitled to a title deed because all mortgages are a charge (lien) against property.

There we are. A mortgage is one of three things: (a) implied conveyance of property to the lender (b) an equitable lien (or charge) on property in favour of the lender or (c) in Quebec, a lien on an immovable.

I like the last definition because that's really what a mortgage is all about.

What's in a Mortgage?

The essential element in a mortgage deed is a covenant to repay the debt, plus interest.

Most basic. The lender puts up the money for one purpose and one purpose only—to obtain a financial return on the investment satisfactory to the lender. An exception to this may be Aunt Sally helping out Cousin Joe, but generally speaking, the name of the game is money. As much as possible, as safely as possible, as securely as possible.

The borrower wants to get the money as cheaply as possible, but mortgage markets being what they are, he hasn't got much choice in the public sector. The private sector is the one where a borrower can pay less for the use of borrowed money, and also where he can get a real hosing and pay the most.

So the mortgagor and the mortgagee reach an agreement as to the size of the loan and its terms and then get formal about it by proceeding with the business of preparing a deed and entering into a legal contract.

A mortgage deed may start right off at the top calling itself an "indenture." The word simply means an agreement between two or more parties, but its history of terminology is interesting.

Many years ago, before carbon paper and all of today's common means of copying, such an agreement would be penned in duplicate (two original copies) and then the copies would be placed evenly, one on top of the other, and a wavy line, or indentation, would be cut along one side of the copies. Each party would receive one and, of course, the idea was that when the two were placed together, the wavy cutting would match. This was supposed to establish authenticity.

Don't tell me. Already you are thinking what fun a slick forger with a new pair of shears could have. At any rate, that's where the word "indenture" came from.

A mortgage to be registered in a land titles office will have the word "charge" on it, so its registry will be easily identifiable.

The names of the borrower(s) and lender(s) will be in it, that's for sure, and a legal description of the property secured as collateral for the loan.

It will clearly state the principal amount of the money *owed* by the mortgagor. You will notice that I did not say the principal amount of the money *borrowed*. One can borrow, say, $9,000 and have a bonus of $1,000 tacked onto it, producing a $10,000 debt, although the borrower never sees the $1,000 bonus until he hands it over to the lender at a later date.

Watch the bonus deals, they can be especially expensive. The borrower not only owes the bonus he never saw, but he pays interest on money that didn't exist for the duration of the loan.

The mortgage will clearly state the rate of interest charged on the loan, but it is here that perhaps the biggest bones of contention exist because of the various means lenders decide to take in extracting the interest. Ensure that your mortgage, if you are the borrower, *clearly* states that the interest will be compounded either annually or semiannually, not in advance, and with no more frequency than that. Many lenders, especially private lenders, will extract interest compounded monthly, which is more expensive. You will find ready reference to all this as you read on.

The term will be there. This is the length of time the borrower has the use of the money (subject, of course, to default in the loan).

The repayment amount will be shown as monthly, quarter-yearly, half-yearly, or annually. It can take many routes, the most common of which are:

(a) A payment covering the interest only.
(b) A fixed payment covering the interest and a portion of the principal amount of the loan.
(c) A fixed principal payment, plus interest.

If a mortgage contains a stated fixed amount at regular intervals to cover "interest and principal" be sure it is large enough at least to cover the interest. Believe it or not, mortgages *are* sometimes thoughtlessly written and when a calculator goes to work on it, it is discovered that the payment actually is a little short of covering the interest!

A court judgement ruled, so I have been told, that in one such mortgage held by the vendor of a property, the vendor's lawyer obtained a court order to have the sale cancelled because, apparently, the effect of the payment not covering the interest was that the vendor had not actually sold the property, but had given the purchaser an option to buy it. Before the purchaser exercised the option, I suppose by rectifying the error, the vendor cancelled the purchaser's rights to the option and got the property back. Read this again and remember it . . .

The responsibilities of the borrower will be spelled out, and basically they are to maintain the payments, keep the property insured, keep the property in a good state of repair, and not misuse it.

The borrower's rights will be shown, such as to have quiet enjoyment of the property and to be free of the lender's rights when the debt is finally paid.

The lender's rights will be shown, and they are quite lengthy. For example, the rights to possession of the property on default by the borrower, and legal recourse to seize the property. These are the most serious. There are many others, such as what happens if the borrower is lazy about paying municipal taxes? The lender can pay them and add the amount to the mortgage debt, plus interest. Ditto for insurance.

One could go on and on about the contents of a mortgage, but the foregoing are the basics. I suggest you obtain a blank copy of a mortgage deed and study it. The document will be a long-winded legal affair, but it is necessary to be legal in detail about such a contract; after all, there is a sizeable amount of money involved.

The mortgage will be signed and witnessed, and everybody will be in business hoping nothing goes wrong.

2
How a Mortgage Is Registered

There are two basic systems of registering real property and mortgages in Canada. I say two *basic* systems, because the Province of Quebec has a system that embraces a part of each of two systems used in the rest of Canada.

In 1763 Great Britain and France ended the Seven Years' War with the Treaty of Paris, but the French inhabitants of North America weren't happy with the newly imposed English Common Law. So King George III agreed to the Quebec Act in 1774 which established the Province of Quebec, an area that included part of what is now Ontario. This Quebec Act stuck with English Criminal Law but allowed the inhabitants to use the French Civil Code and ignore English Common Law.

Well, then along came the American Revolution which found many British subjects immigrating to the Province of Quebec, and these British types didn't go for that French Civil Code business. They wanted the Common Law of Britain.

What to do?

The solution was the Constitutional Act in 1791 which separated the Province of Quebec into Upper and Lower Canada. Upper Canada had English Common Law and Lower Canada had the Civil Code. Everybody seemed happy with the deal.

It was in Upper Canada (later Ontario) on August 10, 1795 to be exact that the first land registry office was established in Canada.

Early registry offices used an alphabetical system to register title and mortgage deeds, but it became a bit cumbersome so this was changed to a system using abstract (history of ownership) books where the documents were registered against lots and plans.

The registry office system with abstract books is a lulu. If it is in your area, and your property is registered there, do a title search sometime and learn what frustration really is. You will hop from page to page and book to book and drive yourself up the wall going to the root of title to your property.

In registry offices nothing is guaranteed. For example, when property changes hands the legal practitioner acting for the purchaser will say in his closing letter that he is of the *opinion* that the title is good and marketable but can't guarantee it.

It is in this registry system that we find the legal mortgages referred to in Chapter 1.

Well, in 1858, in South Australia a man named Robert Richard Torrens came up with an obviously better system of registration for title and mortgage deeds: the government land titles office, which guarantees title documents accepted for registration.

This system today is used in the western provinces, and parts of Ontario. If it is in your area, take a look. You will find everything pertaining to one parcel of property all in one place nice and neat. No jumping from book to book.

Mortgage deeds are registered against title and stamped for time and date. As a matter of fact the first

mortgage recorded in Canada had the time on it—
11 a.m., April 13, 1796.

In the registry office the senior mortgage is the legal
mortgage, as we have discussed. All junior mortgages
are equitable mortgages, the seniority being established by the time and date of registration.

In the land titles office the mortgage is registered as
a charge against title.

In Quebec, a registry office system is used which in
one respect is similar to land titles. The mortgage is a
lien (charge) against title, although no title registration is guaranteed by the Province of Quebec as in
land titles registration.

When you pay off a mortgage, get a discharge certificate from the lender, and ensure that the discharge
of the debt is recorded on title. Otherwise the mortgage registration will just stay there.

It is the lender who registers the mortgage on title,
but it is up to the borrower to remove it.

3
Understanding Amortization

To amortize means to deaden.

To amortize a loan is to extinguish it by means of a sinking fund; in other words, an allowance of payments over a period of time will be made to reduce the debt to zero.

The most common method of amortizing a mortgage is to have the repayment schedule computerized to ensure that all monthly payments are identical, with each payment containing the amortized principal amount, plus interest on the outstanding balance of the loan.

To illustrate this, the following table shows the first year's repayment schedule for a 20-year, $20,000 loan at 10%, compounded seminannually, each line representing one month's payment, and each payment being exactly $190.34.

Payment Number	Interest Payment	Principal Payment	Balance of Loan
1	163.30	27.04	19972.96
2	163.08	27.26	19945.70
3	162.85	27.49	19918.21
4	162.63	27.71	19890.50
5	162.40	27.94	19862.56
6	162.17	28.17	19834.39
7	161.94	28.40	19805.99
8	161.71	28.63	19777.36
9	161.48	28.86	19748.50
10	161.24	29.10	19719.40
11	161.01	29.33	19690.07
12	160.77	29.57	19660.50

In the beginning, each payment is practically all interest. As the loan progresses, each payment contains less interest, and more principal. Each monthly payment still remains the same, with a minor adjustment on the last payment (to take care of the fractions).

Note the allowances for principal payments during the final year of this loan:

Payment Number	Interest Payment	Payment Principal	Balance of Loan
229	17.66	172.68	1989.91
230	16.25	174.09	1815.82
231	14.83	175.51	1640.31
232	13.39	176.95	1463.36
233	11.95	178.39	1284.97
234	10.49	179.85	1105.12
235	9.02	181.32	923.80
236	7.54	182.80	741.00
237	6.05	184.29	556.71
238	4.55	185.79	370.92
239	3.03	187.31	183.61
240	1.50	183.61	.00

One thing to be quite clear about is that regardless of the differences of principal and interest in each payment, the borrower only pays interest on the outstanding principal balance of the loan at the time of each payment. As the loan progresses the borrower is making larger principal payments, because there is less principal on which to pay interest.

If this loan were amortized with equal principal payments, plus interest, this is how the monthly payments would vary:

1st month:	$ 83.33	principal plus
	$163.29	interest ($246.62)
120th month:	$ 83.33	principal plus
	$ 81.64	interest ($164.97)
240th month:	$ 83.33	principal plus
	$ .68	interest ($84.01)

The obvious disadvantage with this method is that the highest payments are in the beginning, when the homeowner probably needs all the available money to support his family.

With rising interest rates, the only possible way to keep monthly mortgage payments down is to lengthen the amortization of the loan.

The following illustrates the repayment of 15, 20 and 25-year amortized mortgages of $50,000, 12% interest compounded twice-yearly.

The table presumes that the mortgage structures will remain constant throughout the loan, which they probably won't, but are used to illustrate the total amount of interest debt possible.

	15 years	20 years	25 years
Monthly payment	$ 590.81	$ 540.49	$ 515.95
Yearly cost	7,089.72	6,485.88	6,191.40
Total cost	106,345.80	129,717.60	154,785.00
Total interest paid	56,345.80	79,717.60	104,785.00

By adding $74.86 to the monthly payment on the 25-year amortization, bringing it down to 15 years, a total of $48,439.20 can be saved.

And reducing the 25-year deal to 20 years by adding $24.54 to each monthly payment, a very respectable $25,067.40 can be saved.

Further savings can be made by *weekly* mortgage payments, which are now available from several big lenders.

Do not confuse the *amortization* of a loan with its *term*. If one is told that a mortgage is amortized for 25 years, it must not be assumed that the loan has a 25-year term. The following chapter will explain.

4
The Mortgage Term

The term of a mortgage is the period of time a borrower has before the lender can demand the principal balance owing on the loan, subject to mortgage default by the borrower.

It is very important to understand this clearly.

Years ago, it was a common practice of lenders to make loans for long periods of time, such as twenty-five years, at a fixed rate of interest for the entire term. But with the shrinking value of our dollar, this ended.

Canada Mortgage and Housing Corporation considered that if it amended the long-term, fixed interest mortgage to one that would allow an adjustment of interest to periods of from one to five years, it would attract more mortgage money.

The amendment was made and other lenders fell in line. With the exception of banks and other large lenders doing business with favored customers, and some private lending, mortgages with a term of more than five years became scarce. Recently, however, seven year terms have surfaced.

There are other reasons for the five-year term.

Trust and mortgage loan companies are offering a prime rate of interest to the public for investing in 5-year certificates and debentures. The trust and mortgage loan firms use the money for mortgage investments at about 2% increase to the mortgagor. The term of such loans most obviously match the term of the certificates—5 years.

If you were the borrower with a repayment schedule amortizing a loan over a period of twenty years, and the mortgage had a five-year term, it would mean that despite the twenty-year amortization, you would have to repay the outstanding principal balance of the loan at the end of five years.

This can be dynamite to your pocketbook.

Take a look at the following table in a $20,000 loan, 9½%, compounded semiannually, amortized over 20 years.

Principal balance owing at end of:

Year	1	$19,640	Year	11	$13,420
Year	2	19,240	Year	12	12,420
Year	3	18,820	Year	13	11,320
Year	4	18,340	Year	14	10,120
Year	5	17,820	Year	15	8,800
Year	6	17,240	Year	16	7,360
Year	7	16,620	Year	17	5,760
Year	8	15,920	Year	18	4,020
Year	9	15,160	Year	19	2,100
Year	10	14,340	Year	20	0

You will notice that in twenty years the loan will be extinguished, but here is where the five-year term will grab you.

At the end of the 5 years, the lender wants his money, namely $17,820. To repay the loan, you probably will have to commit yourself to another mortgage, and borrow the rounded balance of $17,800. If you commit yourself for a further 5-year period (same amortization and rate) this is what your outstanding balance will be over the next 5 years in round figures:

Year 1	$17,479
Year 2	17,123
Year 3	16,749
Year 4	16,322
Year 5	15,859

At the end of this five-year period, when you have to repay the loan, you may repeat the process. We'll do this just twice more, to take us to the end of four five-year terms.

Third five years: ($15,800 loan)		Fourth five years: ($14,000 loan)	
Year 1	$15,515	Year 1	$13,748
Year 2	15,199	Year 2	13,468
Year 3	14,867	Year 3	13,174
Year 4	14,488	Year 4	12,838
Year 5	14,077	Year 5	12,474

Each new five-year term will result in smaller monthly payments because the principal amount of each succeeding term will be less.

If one keeps up the pattern of the five-year terms by starting each new term with the outstanding principal balance of the previous one, and amortizing the loan over twenty-years, it will take more than one hundred years to reduce the loan to zero.

Whereas if the term of the mortgage had been twenty years, it would have been reduced to zero in that time, although the monthly payments would have remained constant (and larger) than under each renewed five-year term.

If the twenty-year mortgage is to be retired, or paid in full in twenty years, then each time the mortgage is renewed, the principal balance owing must be amortized for no longer a period than the remaining number of years in the original amortization.

5
Know Your Interest

Many years ago loans were regarded as forms of help that one owed his neighbour in distress. To profit from his distress was considered to be evil and unjust.

The noun "usury" is from the latin *usura*, meaning the "use" of anything—borrowed capital for example.

About the year 300, usury was defined as "where more is asked than is given," and was prohibited for hundreds of years by the church and state. Usury was considered to be a form of robbery; it still is, but in a different sense.

Pope Eugene III decreed that "mortgages, in which the lender enjoyed the fruits of a pledge without counting them towards the principal, were usurious," and Pope Alexander III declared that credit sales at a price above the cash price were usurious (twelfth century).

However, it was gradually accepted that a loss could occur through lending (the latin verb *intereo* means "to be lost") and that interest was not profit but loss. Thus, interest came to be considered the compensation due to a creditor because of a loss incurred through lending.

This concept derived from Roman law, where it was considered the difference between the lender's present position and that in which he would have stood if he had not loaned.

The term "interesse" became standard early in the thirteenth century.

In early cases, loans were interest-free, but incurred

the penalty of interest if not repaid promptly. Lenders then adopted the practice of charging interest from the beginning of a loan.

For many years, our federal government had condoned the practice of what I considered to be exorbitant interest on money loaned. A prime example of this was the Small Loans Act, which allowed a lender to charge "two percent per month on the unpaid balance" for the first $300 of a loan.

When one desperately needs $100, the cost of paying $2 for its use for a month may not sound unreasonable, but look at it from the lender's side. Two percent per month is 24% per annum. And compounding 24% monthly produces a still higher annual yield to the lender.

The consumer's attitude toward borrowed money is often unrealistic. His first question is: "How much a month will it cost?" The rate of interest is often ignored.

The Small Loans Act no longer exists, but there is a federal limit on what a lender may charge today. Believe it or not, it is *sixty* percent. You will find it in the Criminal Code, but I certainly would not like to hear of any borrower getting into a deal at anything approaching this rate.

Fortunately, even at today's inflated rates, the interest charged on mortgage lending is lower than other forms of financing—lower, for example, than financing an automobile, or financing through the services provided by large department stores, finance companies, or the increasingly popular charging system of the chartered bank.

In Nova Scotia, a Royal Commission on the cost of borrowing money found that one well known finance company charged more than 56% interest on small loans.

In personal loans, the closest one can come to mortgage rates of interest is in loans secured at chartered banks, where the rates charged will fluctuate with the covenant and security of the borrower.

To understand financing, and especially mortgaging, one must have a full understanding of what interest is all about. In many mortgage loans, the borrower pays too much interest on the loan by not understanding how the effective use of interest rates can help. This financing error is not restricted to the "man on the street." Many lawyers and real estate agents, for example, are unfamiliar with the use of interest rates.

There are two types of interest: (a) simple (or fixed) interest and (b) compound interest.

If one borrows money and agrees to repay it plus 10% interest when the loan is repaid, the principal amount of the loan would be repaid plus the 10%, regardless of the repayment date. This is simple or fixed interest—interest on principal (the amount borrowed).

However, if one agreed to repay the loan at 10% interest *per annum*, a loan is immediately created with compound interest, because if the loan is not repaid at the end of the year, the 10% will be added to the indebtedness, and when the loan is repaid at a later date, interest will be paid on the new outstanding balance of the loan, which requires interest to be paid on interest.

If the interest were compounded semiannually, for example, here is how it would look on $1,000 at 10%.

Interest for six months:

$\frac{10\%}{2}$ of $1,000, totalling $50.

Interest for second six months:

$\frac{10\%}{2}$ of $1,050, totalling $52.50.

Interest charge at end of year totals $102.50.

It must be remembered that *the more frequent the compounding, the greater the yield to the lender.* If this interest is compounded quarter-yearly, it will produce $103.81 interest at the end of the year, monthly compounding would yield $104.71.

However, these figures only apply if the loan interest is paid once a year. Not many loans are payable once a year, so to compensate for this, an interest factor (rate) is used to compute the interest to be paid on the loan balance on each payment date.

Interest is not payable in advance and to illustrate this, assume that this loan interest is compounded semiannually, with *interest only* paid once a month.

The interest rate in this case would be .816485%. In other words, $8.16 would be paid each month. Multiplying $8.16 by 12 months produces $97.92, which is what the borrower would actually pay in interest over the 12 months on the 10% loan. Despite the fact that the borrower paid $97.92 over a year, the loan produces an effective annual yield of 10.25% to the lender.

It is called an "effective" yield, because if it were to be an actual yield, there are only two ways it could be accomplished:

(a) If the loan interest were paid once a year.

(b) If the lender immediately reinvested the monthly interest payment to exactly match the loan on which it was paid.

If the lender, receiving the interest monthly, did not reinvest it, he would have just 9.79% to show for his 10% loan at the end of the year. So what the lender actually receives for his investment depends on what he does with his monthly interest payment. If the monthly interest payments were taken out of an old shoe box, the borrower would pay 9.79% for the 10% loan, because money in a shoe box draws no interest.

Interest rates are very easy to establish, providing

the payments are to be made *with the same frequency*. To establish the interest rate on a loan in which the interest is compounded monthly, simply divide the annual rate of interest by twelve. If the interest were compounded quarter-yearly (every three months), divide the annual rate of interest by four, and so on.

However, if one wishes to compound interest, quarter-yearly, for example, and pay the interest monthly, what then? Unless one is a mathematician, a table of interest rates will be needed. Such a table is provided in this book.

Here is an example of how to save money using the interest rates provided. If a loan, for example, stipulates interest at 10% per annum, and no mention is made as to how the interest is compounded, pay it on a basis of annual compounding.

Many borrowers make the mistake of dividing the annual rate of interest by twelve to estimate the interest to be paid for the month. I don't agree with this, unless the interest is compounded monthly. If the loan agreement does not stipulate monthly compounding of interest, don't pay it that way.

Study the tables of interest rates—don't be surprised if you save some money. If you have been paying too much in the past on your loan, the excess can probably be recaptured; business is business.

Recently, a borrower (a corporation) in a large interest-only mortgage agreed to pay the lender on a monthly basis, being 1/12 of the annual rate. The deed did not mention any frequency of calculating the interest, so the borrower later decided the lender was getting too much money.

It sued on the basis that the interest was calculated and paid monthly, saying that it should have been calculated *annually*, and paid monthly. Which, of course, would have cost less.

It lost. The Supreme Court of Canada, noting that

the mortgage said nothing about how the interest was to be calculated, turned down the argument of the deemed reinvestment principle.

On the other hand, here is what Mr. Justice Anglin of the Supreme Court of Canada said in a 1917 judgment concerning mortgages:

"If the rate be stated to be, say 10% per annum, although this is not an explicit statement that the interest is to be computed yearly, such a computation is implied, and I should regard it as a sufficient statement to that effect and as precluding the computation of interest on any other than a yearly basis."

No wonder the average guy out there just says "how much do I pay a month?" and lets others worry about the details!

Calculate:	from the Latin *calculus* which means a pebble or stone used in counting. *Calculus* from the Latin *calx*, which means small pebble. Calculate means compute.
↑ *(synonymous)* ↓	
Compute:	from the Latin *com* which means together, and Latin *puto* which means reckon.
Reckon:	from Old English, Swedish, Danish, etc. which means count.
Compound:	from *compounen* (to put together). Composed of two or more parts; not simple. Synonymous with amalgamation, combination, mixture.
Simple Interest:	That interest which arises from the principal sum only.
Compound Interest:	That interest which arises from the principal with the interest added at stated times, as yearly, twice-yearly, etc. Interest on interest.

6
How Not to Figure a Mortgage Payment

The following is a common error made by many mortgagors (borrowers) when figuring their monthly mortgage payments.

Dividing by twelve!

In mortgages other than conventional loans made by banks, trust companies, etc., the two most common repayment requirements are, for example:

(a) Payment to be $150 monthly, to include principal and interest.

(b) Payment to be $50 monthly off principal, plus interest.

Assume that we are concerned with a $12,000 mortgage loan, at 10% compounded semiannually.

Here is how many borrowers will estimate the first two months' payments under (a):

$$10\% \text{ of } \$12,000 = \frac{1200}{12} = \$100 \text{ interest}$$

Therefore, the payment of $150 will be made up of $100 interest and $50 principal.

At the second month, $50 will be deducted from the loan of $12,000 leaving $11,950 outstanding.

The payment for the second month will be:

$$10\% \text{ of } \$11,950 = \frac{1195}{12} = \$99.58 \text{ interest}$$

Therefore, the payment of $150 will be made up of $99.58 interest, and $50.42 principal.

This system will be repeated throughout the loan.

Under (b) the same system will be used to estimate the monthly interest, but the payments will be constantly smaller because exactly $50 principal will be added to each month's interest payment. In the second payment for example, the $99.58 interest will be added to $50 principal producing a payment of $149.58 for the month.

It will come as a surprise to many borrowers *and* lenders to discover that the first example is entirely *wrong*, and by doing so, the borrower is paying *too much!*

Whenever there is an allowance of principal in a blended mortgage payment, the federal Interest Act requires the mortgage to contain a statement showing the annual rate of interest in the mortgage, "calculated half-yearly, or yearly, not in advance."

Assuming that the mortgage in the example complied with the act, here is why this system of estimating mortgage payments is wrong:

The borrower, by dividing by twelve, is compounding the interest *monthly*, which costs more.

In compounding the 10% interest semiannually, here is what the first two payments should be:

1. $12,000 X the monthly interest factor .816486 = $97.97 interest.

   Therefore, the payment of $150 will be made up of $97.97 interest and $52.03 principal.

2. At the second month, $52.03 will be deducted from the loan of $12,000 leaving $11,947.97 outstanding.

The payment will be:

$11,947.97 X .816485 = $97.54 interest

Therefore, the payment of $150 will be made up of $97.54 interest and $52.46 principal.

By doing it correctly, the borrower, in the first two payments alone, has saved $4.07. Over the term of the mortgage, a consistently greater monthly saving is made by doing it correctly.

Where does the .816485 come from? From the tables of interest rates (Chapter 31). Use them, study them, and save yourself some money.

7
Protecting One's Family

A wise and loving father will have term insurance on his life to at least match the outstanding principal amount of his home mortgages.

This will ensure that in the event of his death, his family will be left with a debt-free roof over its head. A comforting thought!

Could your wife maintain your present mortgage payments? Would your widow be forced to sell the home you shared and fend for herself and your children? Think about it.

We are a nation of procrastinators. Too often the old homestead ends up in other hands after daddy has gone to heaven.

Unfortunately, not everyone can get term life insurance at the drop of a hat. It requires a medical examination, which not all can pass. Then what?

If one wished to borrow $20,000 would it be better getting it from a mortgage lender at 11%, or from a bank at 14%?

In many instances, it would be wiser for the borrower to take the 14% bank loan. Banks offer consumers two loan features that are well worth examining:

• The loan is insured without cost to the borrower.

Which means, of course, that if the borrower should expire, the loan will be automatically paid off and the debt cancelled.

- The loan is "open"; that is, it can be paid off at any time without penalty to the borrower.

The automatic debt-insured bank loan is an excellent feature. It forces one into an act of responsibility at no cost, in that it provides the borrower with needed coverage that may not be otherwise available.

There is no medical examination required to obtain this debt insurance, which is effective the minute one signs on the dotted line. Drop dead three feet from the bank and you're covered.

And the bank's open repayment privilege is a big bonus. Ask a mortage lender what it would cost to pay off a loan before its maturity, and you'll see what I mean.

There are many considerations when shopping for a loan, two absolute musts being life insurance to cover the debt, and the costs of payment before maturity.

The difference between the foregoing examples in the cost of borrowing is 3%. Simple interest on the $20,000 is $600 per year. The bank loan will therefore cost $50 per month more, but consider this: If the borrower could get term insurance to cover the debt, what would it cost? It depends on the borrower's age, so call an insurance agent and do your own arithmetic.

Subtract the answer you get from the bank costs.

Then ask a mortgage lender what it would cost to pay off the loan before maturity.

With the answers to these two points, the $50 a month extra cost to the bank could very well turn into a credit.

Always remember that when committing oneself to a mortgage debt, there is the possibility that before the debt matures an opportunity may present itself to sell the property at a handsome profit — to say nothing of an opportune time.

If the buyer wants the property free of debt, the mortgage lender might turn out to be a monster in his legal demands for repayment. Someone will have to pay the bonus, which will certainly affect the selling price.

So read the mortgage deed carefully before signing it.

And don't forget, if one *can't* get term insurance, and pops off, the bank costs will be peanuts to the estate when reaching the bottom line.

8
The Federal
Interest Act

Now that the long-term mortgage is here with us again, let's not forget the *open* privileges in a *closed* mortgage.

Section 10 (1) of the Interest Act is a bit long winded, but well worth reading in its entirety:

"Whenever any principal money or interest secured by mortgage of real estate is not, under the terms of the mortgage, payable until a time more than five years after the date of the mortgage, then, if at any time after the expiration of such five years, any person liable to pay or entitled to redeem the mortgage tenders or pays, to the person entitled to receive the money, the amount due for principal money and interest to the time of payment, as calculated under sections 6 to 9, together with three months further interest in lieu of notice, no further interest shall be chargeable, payable or recoverable at any time thereafter on the principal money or interest due under the mortgage."

If a borrower signs a mortgage deed with a 10-year term, for example, Section 10(1) says he can repay the

entire balance owing at any time after five years have
expired.

It says the borrower can repay this, but must also
pay three months' interest in *lieu of notice*. What does
this mean?

Reading it, one would logically assume that if, any
time after five years, the borrower gave notice to the
lender that in (say) three months time the outstanding
balance would be paid, no three months' interest
would also have to be paid.

The only cited case to challenge this exact reasoning
was in a district court in Alberta, in 1959, and the borrower was shot down in flames.

The judgment noted that "the lender is held entitled
to three months additional interest to set off against
the probable loss of interest suffered during the period
required to re-invest the fund."

With all the mortgage money available today, this
could be a fact, and not something that may be "probable", but the main thrust of the ruling was in the
grammatical phrasing of the act, which was held to
disallow such a choice for a borrower.

So, the privilege of repayment stands, but along
with it must go three months' additional interest — at
least until another judge rules otherwise.

Now read what section 10 (2) says:

"Nothing in this section applies to any mortgage
upon real estate given by a joint stock company or
other corporation, nor to any debenture issued by any
such company or corporation, for the payment of
which security has been given by way of mortgage on
real estate."

If one buys a parcel of real estate and assumes payments on a long-term mortgage in which a corporation
signed the deed, the five-year break for a borrower
would not apply. Why? Because the corporation sign-

ing the deed places itself under covenant and is responsible for the debt until the bitter end, regardless of who makes the payments.

I am very familiar with Section 10 of the federal interest act. I have written about it, lectured on it, and referred many people to it. It is seared in my brain.

But after all these years, one little item that stands out in Section 10 went right past me. I never caught it. And I'll bet thousands of real estate and mortgage brokers never caught it either.

Laws concerning interest charges go back a lot of years. The first one was a 1777 ordinance in Quebec, which said the maximum will be 6% per annum. This rate was carried into the Upper Canada Act of 1811.

Then the government got generous and the English Act of 1854 repealed the usury statutes and generally left interest rates up to the borrower and lender.

Section 10 (1) of today's interest act is the same as it was in 1925 when a Saskatchewan court of appeal made an interesting observation on it.

Briefly, the section says that when a mortgage has a term of more than five years, the person liable to redeem the mortgage may pay to the lender the amount due for principal and interest at any time after the expiration of five years.

With this payment, the borrower must pay three months' further interest. Then it says no further interest shall be chargeable, payable or recoverable at any time thereafter (on the mortgage).

We have long-term mortgages available now, so this statute, in favour of the borrower, sounds pretty good. Pay off the mortgage after five years with a reasonable bonus and that's the end of the matter.

Not so.

Sixty years ago the honorable court said: "this section does not give a mortgagor entitled to redeem the right to a discharge on tender of the mortgage monies, or interest, after the expiration of five years from the date of the mortgage.

"There is nothing in the section which says he should be entitled to have the mortgage discharged. Ordinarily, if a mortgagee cannot obtain any further interest, he will take his money and execute a discharge of the mortgage. But the section does not say he must do so."

If you think I am digging up ancient history, forget it. This 60-year old precedent was affirmed in 1983 in the B.C. Supreme Court, which said:

"It is difficult to understand what use a mortgagee can make of an instrument where payment is made in full. Nonetheless, if he wishes, it seems he may refuse to discharge the mortgage until the date of its maturity."

All the foregoing suggests that a borrower in a long-term mortgage may be well advised to be polite to the lender. If rates take a dive from a high-rate mortgage, the borrower can certainly take advantage of section 10. But it doesn't guarantee the lender will discharge the mortgage.

Which could be damned annoying if a cash buyer came along for the property: he would want a nice, clean title. If the lender won't hand it over, what is the borrower going to do?

Despite the law, the lender did lose a lot of high-rate interest when that mortgage was paid off before maturity, and he's pretty sore about it. Are we going to find borrowers paying hefty bonuses to get that discharge under such circumstances?

And why wasn't the act amended to take care of this annoying matter? Sixty years is too long to leave some crummy wording on the books!

9
When Can a Mortgage Be Paid Off?

The answer to this question is not clear to many borrowers. There are four types of repayment privileges in mortgage deeds — your mortgage will conform to one of them:

Corporate Borrowers

The Interest Act precludes any prepayment privileges in a mortgage where the borrower is a joint stock company or other corporation, and in any debenture issued by any such company or corporation.

If the mortgage is one with a twenty-year term, the mortgagor is bound to its deed for twenty years. However, if the lender wishes to allow the borrower to repay the loan before its maturity, it is his privilege to do so. This can be written into the deed, or otherwise negotiated.

If the prevailing interest rates at the time of a request to discharge such a mortgage are much higher than the rate in the mortgage, this would probably create no problem. The lender would obviously be glad to have his money returned in order to re-invest it at a higher rate of interest.

Conventional Loans

Here I refer to loans made by such corporations as insurance and trust companies, banks, and other large lenders.

Again the Interest Act applies. Whenver any mortgage is not payable until a time of more than five years after the date of a mortgage (a mortgage with a term of more than five years) the borrower is entitled to repay the principal balance owing at any time after the first five years.

With this prepayment, an additional interest charge equal to 3 months' interest of the mortgage balance is to be made.

The Interest Act states that the balance may be paid in such circumstances "together with three months' further interest *in lieu of notice.*"

One might assume that if a borrower gave the lender 3 months' notice of his intention to repay the loan, no additional interest would be required. But with no guarantee that the borrower will in fact repay the mortgage in three months, such notice is not acceptable by lenders, and the additional interest must be paid.

National Housing Act Loans

Direct funding from CMHC is presently in very short supply, but there is plenty of money available from its approved lenders.

If the mortgage loan is not in default, the borrower has the privilege of paying an additional amount of principal, not in excess of 10% of the original amount of the mortgage, on the first anniversary of the date for adjustment of interest (when the mortgage is one year old).

A similar amount may be paid on the second anniversary date. In each case, three months' interest must be paid on the amount of any such additional payment. These two repayment privileges are not cumulative.

When the mortgage is three years old, and on any instalment date thereafter, the borrower may repay the whole amount owing, or any part of it, together with three months' additional interest on any such additional payment.

"Open" Mortgages

It is quite common for a property owner to accept a mortgage as part of the purchase price of the property he is selling.

The majority of the "purchase mortgages" will contain a clause allowing the mortgagor to pay any part (or all) of the mortgage at any time, or on any payment date, without requiring the borrower to pay any interest penalty.

The obvious reason is that the lender would be delighted to get his money.

In addition to the above, of course, conventional and private lenders can (and often do) insert additional repayment clauses in deeds.

10
The Discharge Certificate

How would you like to have the sale of your house held up because of a debt you paid five years ago?

When a creditor obtains a judgment against a debtor, the judgment is registered with the sheriff's office.

When property is conveyed from one person to another, the last thing checked by the purchaser's solicitor before registration of the deed is the sheriff's records. He wants to be sure there are no outstanding judgments registered against the seller. If there are, they must be cleared off and paid before the property can change hands.

When a judgment is registered with the sheriff, there are two ways to pay it off. Pay the sheriff or pay the judgment creditor.

Paying the sheriff will ensure the judgment is removed — not so paying the creditor.

The creditor registers the judgment but there's no law that says he has to cancel it in the sheriff's office.

If you pay the creditor, ask him to advise the sheriff the debt has been paid. Ask for a copy of his letter to the sheriff. Then check with the sheriff to ensure the debt has been removed. Keep after it.

Why?

Well, suppose you're the debtor. You paid the bill and the creditor didn't advise the sheriff.

Two years later the creditor goes to heaven. Then his solicitor has a heart attack. Then the purchaser's solicitor finds the judgment registered with the sheriff.

Now, if you've lost the proof of payment, why should the sheriff remove it? You have a problem!

And so it is with the mortgage. When it's paid off, the mortgagee or the lender certainly isn't going to see that the deed is removed from the title records. The borrower must do that.

The only costs required a mortgage lender are the nominal charges for registering the mortgage, and sometimes the borrower even pays for that.

So, when you pay off your mortgage, get a mortgage discharge certificate from the lender. Give it to your lawyer and, for a nominal fee, it will be removed from registration against your property.

If this isn't done, it could cause problems years after paying off the mortgage — when you're selling your property.

For example, the lender might have died — or moved. You'll have difficulty convincing a lawyer the debt has been paid. All the buyer knows is the mortgage is still registered.

Say you have some work done on your house and later have a financial dispute with the tradesman. You could find a mechanic's lien registered against the title to your property.

Clouds on title can be downright annoying. Give a man a short option to buy your land and what can happen? Why he could assign his rights to the option to another, who could register the assignment. Now try and get that one removed years later without a few headaches.

For your own peace of mind, check government

records on your own property periodically — just to ensure that everything is a.o.k.

Your property will be registered on one of two ways: In a registry or a land titles office.

Searching title in a land titles office is comparatively simple. Everything pertaining to your own property will be registered in a book in one place.

But not so with the registry office. That's where the frustration begins. You may find yourself jumping from page to page, skipping some and then going into another book. And another.

Take your copy of the title deed to the county records office (in Toronto, at City Hall). They'll tell you where and how to check your own property.

11
Renewing a Mortgage

For years the mortgagor has been doing his best to keep up the payments on the loan, and now the mortgage is nearing the end of its term. This is when a mortgage must be paid off, replaced, or renewed.

Well, most of us can't pay it off, so that's out. Replacing it with a new mortgage from a different lender can be costly and usually means a new set of fees all around. So we logically look to the lender in our present mortgage deed.

If one has a record of making payments on time, or reasonably on time, there will be no problem with large institutional lenders. However, many borrowers have been late with a payment or two or more, and some may have even gone through the traumatic experience of a court action, or something approaching it. Such factors may make one feel that the lender will be reluctant to renew the loan, but this is not necessarily true.

One of the advantages of doing business with a large lender, such as a bank, is that this lender likes to keep a high profile in its public image, plus the fact that it is in business to make money, and therefore it will be reasonable in assessing renewal.

I know of one borrower who had a record of being consistently late in making mortgage payments to a bank, although the payments were always brought up-to-date eventually. The borrower began wondering about the chances of renewal when, one day, about six weeks before the term expiry, an offer from the lender to renew the loan was received in the mail. Right out of the blue and most welcome. Here is how it was handled.

The lender, in assessing the loan, naturally knew of all the late payments, but it also knew that they were brought up-to-date. So it offered to renew the mortgage loan at a rate of ¼ of 1% *above* the rate it would have charged if the borrower had made his payments on time.

The renewal had a face value of about $38,000 which meant, in round figures, that the ¼% increase carried an additional cost of close to $100 a year. The total cost over a 5-year term would be just about what the cost of *replacing* the mortgage would be, so the borrower accepted it. The only other additional cost was a reasonable $30 administrative charge.

If the borrower had had a first-class record of payments, the cost of renewing his mortgage loan would have been just $30, and interest would be at the prevailing rate at the time of renewal. Stick with your present lender if you can — you will probably save money.

With offers of renewal from large lenders, there are options available, such as a reduction in the amount of renewal or possibly an increased amount.

An agreement for a penalty-free mortgage may be obtained by agreeing to pay a higher rate than that offered in the renewal agreement. This means that during the life of the term (usually 5 years) the borrower can make additional lump sum payments to reduce the debt, without being charged an interest penalty. This is worth considering and is simply a matter of arithmetic. The savings could be substantial if one wished to pay off the entire loan before maturity, which normally could be very costly.

If one wished to have a reduced term on the loan, such as 3 years, it would probably be available at *less* than one with a 5-year term.

Also, mortgage debt insurance is usually instantly available covering the life of the mortgagor, reasonably, and without a medical. The insurance payment is made with the monthly loan payment.

The foregoing is what one can expect from large corporate lenders, but what about those "private" mortgages? That's where you take your chances on renewal, unless it is written into the mortgage deed.

One thing to remember about the renewal: Ensure that the *amortization* of the loan does not exceed the remaining number of years in the original loan. Otherwise, you'll never get it paid off.

Here is something for mortgagees and mortgagors to remember:

A common expression of a right to renew a mortgage is "Mortgagor shall have the privilege of renewing this mortgage for a further term of five years upon the same terms and conditions save any further right to renewal." The term, of course, could be for any agreed length of time.

It is often restricted to a condition that the borrower proves to be one of the good ones by never missing a payment. But not always. . . .

How does a borrower renew the loan? Is notice required to be sent to the lender before the first term expires? Is it automatically renewed? Is it done by mailing some post-dated cheques to the lender?

Borrowers and lenders will be surprised to hear what the Ontario Court of Appeal had to say about one option to renew a mortgage:

"Where a mortgage drawn for five years contains a mortgagor's optional right of renewal for one further five-year term unrestricted by any stipulation as to the time in which the option may be exercised and not expressly conditioned upon the mortgagor not being in default, it may be validly exercised by a mortgagor three months after the maturity of the original term."

That decision came, "even though he (the borrower) had been frequently late in making instalment payments and was in default under the mortgage as well as in arrear in his covenanted payments of municipal taxes at maturity."

In a very recent case a lender received no notice before or at the end of a mortgage term saying the borrower is exercising its option to renew the mortgage. So the lender fired off a letter to the borrower saying that in view of receiving no renewal notice, the principal sum, plus accruing interest is "now due and payable."

This mortgage had a clause simply giving the borrower the right to renew, the only restriction being for one further term in the agreement.

The borrower, on the day after receiving the demand for payment, advised the lender it was exercising its right of renewal. The whole thing ended up in the Supreme Court, and the judge agreed with the borrower.

The judgment stated that where "no action had been taken by the lender to enforce payment of the mortgage, the right to renew had not been lost."

"Enforcing payment" would presumably be a court action, which was not done.

The judge noted that: "it will be observed that the

agreement as to renewal is unrestricted as to the time within which the privilege may be exercised and not expressly conditioned otherwise."

It therefore would be in a lender's best interest to be most explicit about when and how a mortgage term may be extended.

This is not to suggest to a borrower that if there is a similar unrestricted renewal clause in a mortgage, the borrower can just relax and renew it any old time.

Remember the rights of the lender. The day after a borrower is late in a mortgage payment, the lender can fire off a writ of foreclosure, which is not only damned costly to the borrower, but it would certainly interfere with any renewal rights that were not exercised — to say the least!

In a power of sale, the lender would have to wait 15 days after default before taking legal action.

So the safest route to take with unrestricted (or any) renewal clauses would be for the borrower to have his lawyer advise the lender (in plenty of time) that the option to renew is being exercised.

The lawyer should specialize in real property law.

PLEASE NOTE: The foregoing time limits for an action of foreclosure and power-of-sale are examples from Ontario Statute law.

12
Why Pay Off a Mortgage?

This question has often come up. A mortgagor has about $20,000 principal balance owing on a mortgage which has not reached the end of its term. A repayment privilege is that it can be repaid at any time without notice or bonus. Now, the mortgagor finds himself with a financial windfall and wonders if he should leave the mortgage alone or pay it off.

That answer is a matter of simple arithmetic. Let us assume that:

(a) The rate of interest in the $20,000 mortgage is 9%.

(b) The mortgagor could safely invest his money at 10%.

Investing $20,000 at 10% produces a round $2,000 annually. The current income tax regulations allow $1,000 of interest income to be tax-free, leaving $1,000 of the $2,000 subject to tax. If one is in a 40% tax bracket, the government will take $400 of this, which will leave a tax free net income of $1,600 on the investment. Sixteen hundred dollars is 8% of $20,000.

So, in this example, one would receive a net return of 8%, and pay the mortgage at 9%, which would cost money. If the mortgage were paid off with the $20,000 there would obviously be a saving.

Take the same example with a $50,000 mortgage, at 9%, and a $50,000 investment at 10%.

Return @ 10%	$5,000
Taxable: $4,000 @ 40%	1,600
Net return on $50,000 investment:	$3,400

Now, the picture is a little bleaker. The net sum of $3,400 represents a return of 6.8%, or less than 7% on the $50,000 investment. The money comes in at about 7%, and goes out at 9%. Obviously, this is going to cost about $1,000 a year right out of the mortgagor's pocket, so the mortgage should certainly be paid off.

The principal consideration here should be: What would you do with the money if you didn't pay off the mortgage? Could it be used to better advantage, possibly to buy some realty or an old masterpiece?

The choice is yours, but if it is a matter of weighing invested capital to produce a fixed return, use the foregoing examples to fit your own particular circumstances, and the answer to the original question will be quite clear to you.

13
The Advantage of Mortgage Acceleration

Mortgage payment acceleration is one of the greatest means available to force oneself to save money.

The example used is a repayment schedule of the first twelve months of a 40-year 10% mortgage loan of $25,250, each monthly payment being $210.41.

Payment Number	Interest Payment	Principal Payment	Balance Owing
1	$206.16	$4.25	$25,245.75
2	206.13	4.28	25,241.47
3	206.09	4.32	25,237.15
4	206.06	4.35	25,232.80
5	206.02	4.39	25,228.41
6	205.99	4.42	25,223.99
7	205.95	4.46	25,219.53
8	205.91	4.50	25,215.03
9	205.88	4.53	25,210.50
10	205.84	4.57	25,205.93
11	205.80	4.61	25,201.32
12	205.76	4.65	25,196.67

When a mortgagor reaches the twelfth payment of this loan, he has the privilege of paying an additional amount of principal, not in excess of 10% of the original amount of the mortgage.

The additional payment made under this privilege is not made in a round figure such as exactly $100. It is a payment that will reach a future balance of the loan. For example, the principal balance owing at payment No. 32 is $25,095.36.

The difference between the balance owing at the twelfth payment and the balance owing at the thirty–second payment is $101.31. By paying the lender this amount, 20 payments of $210.41 each are eliminated. This amounts to $4,208.20.

The chart illustrates the savings that can be effected by making various additional mortgage principal payments at the end of the first year. Further principal payments can be made as outlined in Chapter 9.

Additional Payment	No. of Payments Eliminated	Payment Dollars Eliminated	Balance Owing	Time Left on Mortgage
$101.31	20	$ 4,208.20	$25,095.36	37 yrs., 4 mos.
201.38	37	7,785.17	24,995.29	35 yrs., 11 mos.
301.91	52	10,941.32	24,894.76	34 yrs., 8 mos.
407.48	66	13,887.06	24,789.19	33 yrs., 6 mos.
508.04	78	16,411.98	24,688.63	32 yrs., 6 mos.

14
Your Mortgage Covenant

What does it mean when you sell your house and the buyer agrees to "assume" the existing mortgage?

It's important for the house seller to be fully aware of his own responsibilities to a lender when this is done.

How would you like to be served with a writ charging you with a few thousand dollars in mortgage arrears two years after you sold your house?

Don't think it can't happen!

The one who signed the mortgage deed is responsible for the debt until it is paid. Period.

You put your house on the market. A buyer likes the mortgage registered against the property, so he agrees to pay "cash to mortgage" and further agrees to assume the mortgage.

Now, stop right here and remember this.

What the buyer is really saying is that he will continue making the payments on the mortgage.

But a very important point to remember is that the lender in the mortgage deed, the mortgagee, does not legally agree with this.

When you obtained the loan, the lender checked your credit rating and your ability to repay the money. The agreement under the mortgage is with you and the lender. No one else.

So after you have sold the property and conveyed your equity and title deed to the buyer, you are still responsible for the mortgage debt.

If the buyer continues to make the payments on time, there is no problem.

But if the buyer purchased the property with a modest down payment, and defaulted under the mortgage, the lender could go after the property — and you — under a power of sale.

If, by some freak in the market, the sale didn't cover the mortgage debt, the lender could go after you for the balance owing.

If your buyer sold the property and his buyer agreed to maintain the mortgage payments, your buyer is off the hook and the second buyer is now in the picture.

And so are you. You are always there until the mortgage is paid off, or until the lender agrees to accept someone else's covenant for security. Then you're home free.

When there is a substantial amount of cash involved in the sale, don't worry about it. No buyer is going to walk away from a chunky down payment.

But sometimes properties are sold that have mortgage debts which come close to the sale price. It's here one may be forgiven for keeping fingers crossed praying nothing goes wrong.

If you help with the sale by taking back a second mortgage from the buyer, think carefully about the size of the loan. If the buyer gets the property with about 5% down, a quick recession could wipe out its market equity.

Then, if your buyer sold the property, possibly because of circumstances beyond his control, you may have a problem. The first mortgage and your second just cover the market value of the real estate.

When lending a buyer money this way, check the

buyer's credit rating, his ability to repay the loan, stability of work record and character. If you are satisfied about all this, you can breathe easier about it.

It is common practice today to find two clauses in mortgage deeds. One says if the property is conveyed, or sold to another, the mortgage must be paid off.

The other is that if the lender approves of the property buyer, the mortgage may be assumed by the buyer if he passes a credit check. Also, the lender may require the new guy to pay an adjusted market rate of interest.

But only if the interest is currently higher than that in the mortgage deed. Naturally.

Those lenders are getting smarter every day. . . .

15
The Postponement Clause

This short chapter can save many headaches.

Remember, mortgage seniority is established by the time and date of registration in a land registry office or land titles office.

If one becomes a borrower in a second mortgage, and the term of his second mortgage has a longer period of time to run than the existing first mortgage on the property, what happens when the first mortgage becomes due?

When such a situation occurs, the first mortgage cannot be renewed or replaced without the express permission of the one holding the second mortgage.

This could mean trouble.

If there are two mortgages on a property, it is unlikely that the mortgagor would have the funds to pay off the larger first mortgage and allow the second to take its place.

There is only one solution.

The second mortgage must contain a postponement clause, which would automatically allow the mortgagor to renew or replace the first mortgage when it becomes due.

This does not mean that a $10,000 first mortgage can be increased to $15,000 with the borrower putting the $5,000 in his pocket.

Any increase in the principal amount of a first mortgage being renewed or replaced under these circumstances would be paid to the second mortgagee to reduce his mortgage.

Know the mortgage expiration date and remember the postponement clause.

16
Costs of Arranging a Mortgage

Many real estate buyers receive their indoctrination into the realm of financial shock upon receiving the final bill for charges and services rendered. A review of letters I have received from coast to coast strongly indicates that *caveat emptor* (let the buyer beware) truly prevails, and the chief complaint appears to be that "nobody told us."

There are financial charges in obtaining a mortgage loan, which are paid by the borrower. These charges amount to hundreds of dollars which the unsuspecting borrower knows nothing about until he gets the bill. This is written to reveal how you can avoid many or even *all* of them.

The two most misunderstood charges to a real estate buyer are the legal fees in obtaining a mortgage loan, and the insurance fee added to many mortgages.

A lawyer is entitled to reasonable compensation for his services, and considering the work involved in acting for a purchaser, the generally accepted tariff appears to be fair.

In acting for a purchaser, there is one necessary aspect of the lawyer's work that surely must drive some of them "up the wall." That is when a property is registered in a registry office.

In a land titles office (not used east of Ontario) all title documents registered are guaranteed by the provincial government, but not so in the registry office. Hours and hours of patient sifting through abstract books can be required, going from page to page and book to book, the lawyer all the time being acutely aware that there just might be something wrong in the chain of title that will interfere with the client's enjoyment of the property at a later date.

The legal fees in acting for a purchaser can amount to about 1¼% of the cost of the average home. This is for the lawyer's services, and in addition to this, there will be adjustments to the date of closing made on such things as the municipal property taxes, hydro and water charges, insurance, and if oil heated, the cost for a full tank.

Then there will be a charge for a land transfer tax, which the provincial government gets.

There will be a charge made by the registry offices for every document registered. If the property covers parts of more than one lot, it costs more.

Some mortgage lenders will deduct a portion of future municipal taxes from the mortgage principal, which can be annoying to one's pocketbook, resulting in more cash to be coughed up by the buyer. Also, many mortgage lenders require an up-to-date survey and, if one is not available, this can cost hundreds of dollars.

Then there will be a final check made with the sheriff's office to see if any last minute liens or charges have been made against the property, for which there will be a nominal charge.

The average buyer, after paying for much of the foregoing, can be forgiven if he finds himself in a state of shock upon being presented with an additional bill for third party mortgage charges. The following are the three basic areas of financial escalation in mortgaging costs for the borrower and will clearly indicate just how you can save money in mortgaging.

A common method of mortgaging in buying real estate is for the purchaser to "assume" an existing mortgage, one already registered against the property. The one assuming the mortgage is agreeing basically to maintain the payments and be jointly responsible for the debt with the one who originally signed the mortgage deed.

Assuming a mortgage when buying real estate normally incurs no extra financial charges to the buyer; it is already there.

Another method is for the seller to agree to "take back" a mortgage from the purchaser for part of the purchase price. This is another cheap way to get a mortgage.

Such a mortgage has several advantages. It requires no credit check of the borrower, no appraisal fees to be paid by the borrower, smaller legal fees than other mortgaging, instant knowledge that the "mortgage application" has been approved, and in many cases can be secured at a lower rate than third party mortgages, with longer terms. Furthermore, they usually have "open" repayment privileges.

The most expensive method of mortgaging is for a purchaser to arrange a mortgage from a third party, such as a bank, insurance, or trust company.

Charging an inspection fee of about $75.00 does not seem unreasonable, but the big financial crunch comes when a lawyer presents his bill for legal fees and disbursements. In a typical, recent $18,400.00 mortgage, the borrowers were charged $28.50 for disbursements, and $235.00 for legal fees, for a total of $263.50!

Legal tariffs in mortgaging can be just as much proportionately as they are for services in closing the purchase. The reason for this is that many of the services performed in mortgaging are identical to services in closing. For the lender's protection, the title must be searched in the same manner, right down to a last minute visit to the sheriff's office.

Lending institutions usually prefer to retain the services of their own approved lawyers, which is understandable. This results in a complete job being done in the title search, etc., in addition to the one done by the purchaser's lawyer for closing purposes. Result—the additional fee.

If a purchaser is fortunate enough to have his own lawyer do the legal work in the third party mortgage, the combined fee for mortgaging and closing will undoubtedly be much less than the separate fees of two lawyers. It therefore follows that it can be advisable for a purchaser to determine what lawyer will be acting for the mortgage lender and also retain him to close the purchase. Or better still, have one's own lawyer arrange for the funds through a lender who will allow him to act in the mortgage.

One thing to keep in mind is that the mortgagee (lender) pays for absolutely nothing, with the exception of a small charge for registering the mortgage. The borrower pays all costs for the simple reason that if the lender paid for any part of it, his investment would be "watered down." When a lender advances money at 10% he wants 10% and he *gets* 10%.

The second puzzling charge confronting a borrower is the mortgage insurance fee. This charge is found in two types of mortgages: National Housing Act loans and loans insured by the Mortgage Insurance Company of Canada.

When a mortgage is obtained that amounts to no more than 75% of the value of the property, it is generally accepted that there is sufficient equity in the property to require no monetary insurance.

But when the loan amounts to as much as 90% of the purchase price, it is understandable for the lender to consider that the borrower, having a 10% equity in the property, is a risk that requires additional assurance that the loan will be secure. This assurance is realized by having the loan completely insured in favour of the lender. The borrower pays the premium, plus an underwriting fee.

The insurance premium is not normally paid for directly out of the borrower's pocket. It may be added to the principal amount of the loan, and the total will be the registered principal sum in the mortgage deed, although MICC will accept a direct payment.

The lender then sends a cheque matching the premium to the insurer, CMHC, or MICC. If the mortgage is paid before the mortgage term expires, there is no provision for any rebate of the insurance premium.

Regardless of the source of mortgage funds, the lender will require the borrower to have the security adequately covered by property insurance. It is mandatory, written into the mortgage deed, and paid for by the borrower.

Consider very carefully how mortgaging is going to affect your pocketbook. The young couple who were the borrowers in the $18,400.00 mortgage deed were hit with mortgage charges which they did not expect or understand. Nobody told them.

Caveat emptor.

In summary, consider the following:

(a) Property where there is a mortgage already registered at current rates or lower. If you can't come up with cash to the mortgage, see if the vendor will hold a second at a reasonable rate of interest.

(b) Property where the vendor will take back a mortgage for a large part of the purchase price.

(c) If you must go to a third party for a mortgage, retain the mortgagee's lawyer to close your purchase, or have your lawyer act for the mortgagee (lender) if possible.

(d) Be wary of short term mortgages that have to be replaced. They can be expensive.

17
Canada's National Housing Act

Canada's federal government has been involved in housing development since the depression.

In 1935, the Dominion Housing Act was passed, principally as a means of providing jobs, but also to help improve the quality of Canadian housing and to establish building standards.

Under the Dominion Housing Act, the federal government provided one-quarter of the money for high-ratio mortgages with private lenders providing the balance. The objective was to make it easier for people to build and buy houses by supplying bigger mortgages—and make possible smaller down payments than would be available from private lenders.

Between 1935 and 1938, about 5,000 new houses were put up with financing provided in part under the Dominion Housing Act. Then, in 1938, the first act was replaced with the new National Housing Act which provided more mortgage money and which, for the first time, offered loan assistance for the construction of housing for low-income families.

But the federal government really didn't come into its own in the housing field until World War II. Housing starts fell off during the war, so when hostilities ended, there was an enormous backlog of demand. To help meet this demand, a new National Housing Act was passed in 1945.

Central Mortgage and Housing Corporation, a Crown Corporation, put up 17,000 new houses for veterans and took over ownership of all other wartime housing so that, by 1949, the government agency owned 41,000 houses. Most of these wartime houses have since been sold to former tenants.

Under the 1945 National Housing Act, postwar housing construction entered a real boom period. In the early years, lots of private money also was available for mortgage financing. Canada's output rose from 64,400 new houses in 1946 to 92,350 in 1950, when almost half of the year's total production was financed under NHA.

By the early fifties, however, private mortgage money sources began to dry up; the boom had been so explosive that most "conventional" money was fully committed. So in 1954 the National Housing Act was again overhauled, this time establishing a system of insurance of NHA mortgages so that these mortgages became an attractive alternative to bonds as long-term investments. Under this system, the full amount of the mortgage was provided by a private lender and the government guaranteed, first 98%, and finally the full loan amount (the borrower paid the insurance fee that provided this guarantee). In this way the government for a while stopped actually lending money, except as a last resort, for housing and simply made it 100% safe for private lenders to provide the funds.

At around the same time, the Bank Act was changed so that, for the first time, the chartered banks were allowed to make long-term mortgage loans. This increased available funds for home building tremendously.

By 1958 the number of housing starts in Canada had risen to the unprecedented total of 164,000.

Since then things have become more difficult for builders and buyers alike. Land costs, wages, and materials have all risen, driving the price of new houses up, to say nothing of rising interest rates.

Because the banks were limited by law to charging 6% interest, they virtually stopped putting money into NHA mortgages in 1959 when interest rates started rising. The other lenders—life insurance, trust, and loan companies—still had money to put into mortgages, but they put more and more into higher-paying, private mortgages, less into the low-paying NHA variety.

So, although housing starts reached an all-time record of 166,565 in 1965, the supply of private money for mortgages began to dwindle away.

To keep the industry going and to put roofs over Canadians' heads, the government changed the Bank Act again to allow the bank to lend mortgage money at interest rates higher than 6%. Even more significantly, the government has pumped vast amounts of public money directly into housing as private funds started staying away. By 1967, the federal government was holding, through CMHC, about three *billion* dollars worth of mortgages.

During the past few years further amendments were made to the act, and today the help provided by CMHC is varied and extensive. Here are the current provisions for home ownership loans.

The down payment must be within your financial means and the monthly payments on your mortgage plus municipal taxes and other continuing charges such as heat, electricity, maintenance costs (and condominium costs, where applicable) should be covered comfortably by your housing budget. Whether you build or buy your new or existing home, the financing terms and conditions will be the same.

NHA Loans

National Housing Act loans are available for the purchase of a newly built home or the purchase and improvement (if required) of an existing dwelling.

The type of dwelling that may be bought or improved includes a single-detached house, a unit of row housing, a duplex, a unit in a condominium, or one or both units of a semi-detached dwelling. Cooperative housing associations wishing to purchase new or existing housing projects may also obtain NHA loans.

Loans may also be made to builders for the construction of houses for sale or for financing houses acquired as "trade-ins" which are to be resold to a buyer who intends to occupy the dwelling. The buyer makes a down payment to the builder and assumes responsibility for repayment of the mortgage.

Types of NHA Loans

Approved Lender Loans: The National Housing Act provides for loans by approved lenders. These are private companies such as chartered banks, life insurance companies, and trust and loan companies authorized by the federal government to lend under the terms of the act. A list of these companies is available from any Canada Mortgage and Housing Corporation office.

Direct Loans: Direct Loans from CMHC are available only in those areas not normally serviced by approved lenders. For information regarding your particular locality, you should discuss your requirements with the nearest office at CMHC.

Loan Amount

The amount of a loan one may obtain will depend on the "lending value" of the property, the maximum loan permitted, and your annual income.

Lending value is the value of your proposed house and lot as established by CMHC. The lending value for mortgage purposes is not necessarily equal to the actual price of the property.

As a general guide, annual payments to be made for principal and interest on the loan, and for municipal taxes, heating costs and 50% of condominium fees, if applicable, should not exceed 32% of the borrower's annual gross income. In establishing this gross income, the lender may consider a portion, or all, of the income of one's spouse.

Cash Requirements

A borrower will have to provide a downpayment equal to the difference between the NHA loan and the total cost of the house and lot. The minimum requirement, 10% of the lending value, must come from the borrower's own resources.

If one cannot provide this total in cash, the amount in excess of the 10% minimum may be borrowed from other sources only if the repayment, when combined with the mortgage payment, does not exceed 32% of the borrower's gross income.

If the borrower already owns a building lot, its value will reduce the cash requirements, as will the value of any labour one plans to do on the home.

Interest Rate

The interest rate for loans made by approved lenders

is negotiable between borrower and lender, but must be within current market ranges.

Taxes

Under NHA arrangements, your monthly payment to the lender includes an amount equal to one-twelfth of the estimated annual taxes on your home.

When you receive your tax bill from the municipality, you forward it to your lender for payment. Some lenders arrange with the municipality to have tax bills sent directly to them for payment and then mail the receipted bill to the homeowner.

The monthly amounts collected are based on an estimate of your taxes for the year ahead. Where taxes prove to be higher or lower than the estimated amount, the lender will adjust the tax portion of your monthly payment accordingly.

Repayment of Loan

Most NHA loans are made on a one- to five-year basis, with repayment amortized over a period of 25 years.

The interest rate and related monthly mortgage payments will be constant for one to five years, after which the borrower must renegotiate the interest rate with the lender. Monthly payments will then be adjusted to reflect the new interest rate.

Prepayment of Loan

After you have made 36 regular monthly payments, you may pay off all or part of the balance owing on your loan. At the time of the twelfth and twenty-fourth payments you may make a prepayment of not more than 10% of the original loan amount. Whenever prepayments are made, your lender may ask for a three months' interest bonus on the amount paid off in advance. Any prepayments you make will, of course, reduce the amount of interest charges on your mortgage loan and, without altering the monthly payments, will reduce the repayment period.

Application for Loan

Formerly, a loan application could not be approved if work had gone beyond the first floor joist (including subfloor) stage of construction for one and two-unit houses.

Now, applications can be approved if work has gone beyond the first floor joist when units are registered to New Home Warranty programs and NHA standards, or equivalent are enforced by the municipality.

There will be an application fee.

Mortgage Insurance Fees

All NHA approved lenders are insured against loss on the loans they make through the operation of a Mortgage Insurance Fund established under authority of the act. A table of current charges follows:

LOAN SIZE (as a percentage of property value)	PREMIUM* EXISTING HOUSING	NEW HOUSING
75% or less	1.0%	1.5%
more than 75% to 80%	1.5%	2.0%
more than 80% to 85%	2.0%	2.5%
more than 85% to 90%	2.5%	3.0%

NOTE: There is a 1.0% surcharge for new construction of condominiums.

Insurance of this type must not be confused with mortgage life insurance which provides for payment of the outstanding balance in case of death of the borrower. Mortgage life insurance may be obtained from insurance agents and, quite commonly, from large lending institutions.

Other Charges

In addition to the application fee and mortgage insurance fee, the approved lender may deduct from your loan, or bill you for costs involved in obtaining a surveyor's certificate or its equivalent showing the location of your house on the lot, and for legal work performed for the lender. You will also be required to pay the accumulated interest on mortgage advances made during construction.

Start of Construction

It is a condition of loans under NHA that a construction stage inspection be requested within six months of approval of the loan.

Loan Advances

Construction of your house may be started when your loan has been approved. The loan will be disbursed to you in progress advances as work proceeds, or in a single advance on completions as requested by the lender.

The amount of each advance is based on the percentage of work completed.

Inspections

While your house is being built, a number of construction inspections will be made by CMHC. These are not full architectural or engineering inspections; they are made to protect the investment of the lender by ensuring that the house is built in reasonable conformity with the plans and specifications, and housing standards prescribed by CMHC.

They may also serve to check construction progress of loan advances.

18
The High-Ratio Mortgage

Prior to 1964, a Canadian buying a house with a conventional mortgage had to come up with either one-third of the value of the house and lot in cash or put down less cash and assume, or obtain, a second mortgage. This second mortgage usually carried a fairly high rate of interest and involved additional legal costs.

Consequently, many were unable to realize their dream of owning their own home. In 1964, conventional high-ratio mortgages, jointly funded by a regulated lending institution (i.e., an insurance company, trust company or loan company) and a non-regulated mortgage investment company, and insured by The Mortgage Insurance Company of Canada (the first private sector mortgage insurance company in Canada), became available and the picture changed dramatically. Initially, first mortgages were available up to 83⅓% of value and subsequently to 87½%. For six years, until 1970, variations and refinements made the high-ratio mortgage an important part of the housing scene.

In March of 1970, amendments to the Canadian and British Insurance Companies Act, the Foreign Insurance Companies Act, the Trust Companies Act, and the Loan Companies Act were passed by the

Parliament of Canada. Under these amendments, lending institutions operating under these Acts, as well as the chartered banks, were authorized to make mortgage loans over 75% of value (using all of their own funds) provided the excess was insured by a policy of mortgage insurance, issued either by a federal or provincial government or agency thereof, or an insurance company registered under the Canadian and British Insurance Companies Act.

In 1973, the private mortgage insurance industry expanded with the creation of two other companies, the Sovereign Mortgage Insurance Company and Insmor Mortgage Insurance Company. These companies merged in 1977 and Insmor carried on in the business. Late in 1981, Insmor and MICC merged, leaving The Mortgage Insurance Company of Canada as the only private mortgage insurer in Canada.

Since 1964, more than 500,000 families have bought their own home, using the MICC insured high-ratio mortgage plan. Under this plan, the mortgage lender is provided with substantial protection against loss in the event the borrower does not make his mortgage payments, and the homeowner is able to purchase a home with a modest downpayment.

Using an MICC high ratio mortgage, a house may be purchased with as little as 10% down to one 90% mortgage. The loan amount obtainable is based on a formula as follows:

90% of the first $80,000 of value
plus
80% of value in excess of $80,000

A mortgage insurance premium is payable by the borrower. It does not have to be paid in cash, but may be added to the mortgage. The premium varies with the loan amount, the loan-to-value ratio and the term of the policy. Also, it is ½ of 1% higher for mortgages secured by newly constructed homes than for existing properties. Following is the premium structure for a high-ratio mortgage on an existing house for the type of coverage usually required by lenders:

Loan to Value Ratio	Policy Term	Premium
75% - 80%	20 years	1½% of loan amount
80% - 85%	20 years	2% of loan amount
85% - 90%	20 years	2½% of loan amount

MICC also offers a range of other coverages to lenders at varying premium rates.

The following example illustrates the loan amount available, downpayment required and the mortgage insurance premium payable for a typical case:

Home Value (existing property)	$80,000
Basic loan amount available =	
90% × $80,000 =	$72,000
Downpayment required	$8,000
Mortgage insurance premium =	
2½% × $72,000 =	$1,800
Total mortgage	
(unless premium paid in cash)	
Basic mortgage	= $72,000
Mortgage insurance premium	= $1,800
TOTAL MORTGAGE	= $73,800

MICC high-ratio mortgages are available to finance the purchase of a new or existing home, to finance the construction of a new home for sale or occupancy, and to refinance an existing mortgage to obtain cash, consolidate debts, or carry out home improvements.

Eligible properties include detached houses, semi-detached properties, duplexes, triplexes and units in condominium projects. There is no minimum market value or maximum age limit for a house to qualify. Homes built prior to 1950 will be expected to be substantially modernized: e.g., new heating system, renovated bathroom and kitchen, improved insulation, etc. New houses must conform to the National Building Code and the Residential Standards Canada or the applicable municipal or provincial building codes. All new housing for sale must be covered by the applicable provincial or regional New Home Warranty Program.

High-ratio mortgages are available in all of Canada's major cities and communities constituting part of their market territory. Further information regarding communities where the MICC insured program is available may be obtained from The Mortgage Company of Canada.

The interest rate on an MICC insured high-ratio mortgage today, all across Canada, is generally the going rate of interest on conventional mortgage loans.

The borrower makes application to the mortgage lender in the usual way and there is a complete lack of red tape, and no special procedures to be involved. The low downpayment makes buying easier. The larger mortgage amount also makes selling easier, should the homeowner decide to move.

The advent of the insured high-ratio mortgage has opened up the housing market to a large number of Canadians who have difficulty saving a large downpayment or who were unwilling, or unable, to pay the high interest rates demanded on most second mortgages. Thousands of homeowners would undoubtedly be still paying rent, unable to enjoy the pride of ownership of their homes, if it were not for this facility.

Present high house prices and high interest rates make it difficult for some, and impossible for others, to buy. Land costs, labor costs, interest rates, and house prices will no more return to levels of the past than will the costs of autos, hamburgers, or golf balls. However, we can hope that items making up the end price of housing will stabilize, perhaps even ease somewhat. We can also hope that items such as mortgage interest rates, which affect the carrying costs of housing, moderate as inflation eases.

Most mortgage lenders follow the general rule that a borrower should not commit himself to pay more than 27% to 30% of his gross salary for his mortgage payments and taxes. (If a borrower has no other debts a higher ratio may be accepted.) This ratio is called the Gross Debt Service Ratio (GDS ratio).

A portion of the spouse's income may be used, depending on her age and the stability of her employment.

> *Example*
> Gross monthly income = $1,750.00
> 27% = $472.50
> 30% = $525.00

Therefore, a person with an income of $1,750 a month (before deductions) should normally not pay more than $472.50 to $525.00 per month on his/her mortgage, including taxes.

The lender also looks at the borrower's other debts, credit rating, and so on when reviewing a mortgage application. The general rule is that the borrower should not commit himself/herself to pay more than

37% to 40% of his/her monthly gross income to his/her mortgage payment (including taxes) and the monthly amount to be paid on other bank loans, finance company loans, etc. This ratio is referred to as the Total Debt Service Ratio — TDS ratio.

In order to determine the amount of mortgage that a borrower can afford, the amount of his/her income that can be committed to his/her monthly mortgage payment must be established using the GDS and TDS guidelines above. Assume that the amount available for the mortgage and taxes payment is $500 and taxes are $75 per month; the amount then available to cover mortgage principal and interest is $425 per month. What amount of mortgage will a payment of $425 per month repay?

A schedule of monthly payment factors is now required to assist in determining the mortgage amount. This schedule indicates the monthly payment required to pay off, or amortize, a mortgage of $1,000 at various rates of interest over varying numbers of years. Assume that you can obtain a mortgage at 11½% on a 25-year repayment plan. The monthly payment factor is $9.97 per month per $1,000 borrowed. Then $425 per month would handle a mortgage of:

$$\frac{\$425}{9.97} \times \$1,000 = \$42,627$$

Application for a high-ratio mortgage loan is made in the normal way to any MICC approved lender (i.e., banks, trust companies, credit unions, life insurance companies, savings and loan companies, caisses populaires.)

In addition to insuring high-ratio mortgages on homes, MICC also insures mortgages on income producing properties such as apartment buildings, shopping centers, office buildings, etc. Details are available from MICC on request.

For a complete list of approved lenders, and detailed information on this service to homebuyers, write to:

THE MORTGAGE INSURANCE COMPANY OF CANADA
1 Dundas Street West, Box 12, Suite 1600
Toronto, Ontario
M5G 1Z3

19
How to Buy a Mortgage

The most common mortgages bought and sold are "second" mortgages. There is no mystery about them and they are, if properly purchased, a sound and profitable investment. Before buying one, however, there are a few guidelines to follow to help one arrive at not only a sensible decision about which one to buy, but also to ensure that the price is right!

The four prime areas that require scrutiny are (a) the real estate used as security, (b) the equity in the property, (c) the covenant, or the ability of the mortgagor (borrower) to repay the loan and (d) the details of the mortgage terms.

Whenever a mortgagee (lender) is asked to loan money, the property involved will be inspected and appraised to ensure that there is sufficient tangible security for the loan. The mortgagor pays for the inspection.

In considering the purchase of second mortgages one cannot very well have an appraisal done on all the real estate involved. This would require a fee to be paid for each mortgage considered.

The alternative is for the mortgage purchaser to inspect the property himself. In this inspection, it is wise to check not only the condition of the building carefully, but also to note how the title holder (owner) is maintaining it.

Regardless of any documents produced to show evidence of what the current market value of the property is, the mortgage purchaser should, if possible, make comparisons and inspect properties that are offered for sale in the same area that are of a similar plan and size to the one secured by the mortgage.

Also, check with the hydro authority, municipal buildings department, and registry office to see if there are any outstanding work orders issued against the property. If there are, the work will have to be done, and the cost of repairs or renovations must be considered in the value.

Mortgage seniority is established by the time and date of registering the mortgage deed. A second mortgage ranks second, so that the mortgage of first priority has first claim to the dollar value of the security.

Other, more junior mortgages may be registered against the property, but the second mortgage will take precedence over these.

The equity in a property is its market value, less the total amount of all mortgages and other financial charges registered against the property. It is therefore important to know something about the mortgagor and his ability to repay the loan, because his only stake in the property is this equity.

If there is very little equity, it does not necessarily mean that the mortgagor will be any more lax in his payments than one with a larger equity, but regardless of the tangible security, a mortgagee likes to have some reasonable assurance that the debt is going to be paid, and paid according to contract.

The financial decision in purchasing a second mortgage must be based on two prime factors: (a) the rate of interest, and (b) the terms of the loan.

Second mortgages, having a secondary position, normally require a higher rate of return than first mortgages. If the current rate of interest, for example, is 14% on secondary financing, then the rate in the mortgage considered must be adjusted accordingly.

The hardheaded mortgage buyer will demand it, and his rule of thumb method of rapid calculation will be: Assuming the rate of interest on an existing second mortgage is 9%, and one wishes to have it produce 14%, the 5% difference will be multiplied by the number of years remaining in the term of the mortgage, or to its maturity, when the principal balance is due and payable. The result will be the discount at which he will purchase the mortgage. Some illustrations are shown in the chart.

By purchasing a mortgage in this manner, two obvious bonuses will be secured: (a) the additional interest extracted from the mortgage is obtained in advance and (b) this additional interest is based on the present outstanding principal balance of the mortgage, and not on a reducing balance which occurs as the loan payments progress.

Example of One Method Mortgage Buyers Use in Discounting Second Mortgages

Mortgage Principal	Rate of Interest	Interest Required	Difference	Mortgage Term	Discount
$2,000.00	10%	14%	4%	3 years	12% ($ 240)
3,000.00	9%	15%	6%	4 years	24% ($ 720)
4,000.00	8%	13%	5%	5 years	25% ($1000)
5,000.00	10%	14%	4%	2 years	8% ($ 400)

To know the *exact* price one should pay for a mortgage to produce a specific yield, you must get a computerized analysis available from many computer services.

If you are *selling* a mortgage, it is also important to

obtain an accurate market valuation of the mortgage. Don't sell it for anything less than you have to. The foregoing illustrations are not precisely accurate, and are used only as a rough guide to illustrate discounting.

Remember this: If you are going to be a mortgagee in a purchase mortgage with the intention of selling it, keep the interest rate as close as possible to current market rates, and the term down to three years if possible.

20
Mortgage Repayment Schedules

There are more than *one million* new and refinanced mortgage transactions each year in Canada.

Conventional mortgagees such as banks, insurance, and trust companies provide the borrower with a computerized repayment schedule showing the interest and principal parts of each payment, and the principal balance owing on each payment date. This ensures that the borrower and the lender each know exactly where they stand, right to the penny.

However, in many areas of mortgaging, and especially secondary financing, millions of dollars is undoubtedly being lost annually by borrowers simply because the mortgage repayment is not computerized.

The following is an example which illustrates why under normal circumstances, it is incorrect to compute an interest payment on a level balance over six months.

Calculated vs. Compounded

The statement of interest in most mortgages may read, for example, "6% per centum per annum calculated half-yearly not in advance."

Note: It is the *interest rate* which is calculated half-yearly *not* the *interest payment*.

In most cases the interest payment is due monthly with the principal. The word "calculated" does not imply that the interest payments are computed on a level balance over six months. In fact, the following shows it is quite incorrect to compute interest payments in this way.

Interest Paid Monthly for Six Months vs. Interest Paid on a Level Balance Over Six Months

Suppose for example, a mortgage of $10,000 with interest at 6% per annum calculated half-yearly, is to be paid off in equal instalments of $100 interest and principal included. The 6% per annum interest rate calculated semiannually is equivalent to a monthly interest rate of 0.4938622%. The first 6 rows of schedule will read as follows:

Payment Number	Interest Portion	Principal Portion	Total Payment	Balance of Loan after Payment
1	49.39	50.61	100.00	9949.39
2	49.14	50.86	100.00	9898.53
3	48.88	51.12	100.00	9847.41
4	48.63	51.37	100.00	9796.04
5	48.38	51.62	100.00	9744.42
6	48.12	51.88	100.00	9692.54
Total	292.54	307.46	600.00	

On examining the schedule you will note that the sum of the interest on the first 6 payments is $292.54 whereas the interest of $10,000.00 for half a year at 3% is $300.00. The difference arises because the principal is being reduced by a portion of the monthly instalments as the amount of interest decreases within the 6 month period.

It would be improper under the Interest Act for the lender to compute the balance due after the sixth payment by simply adding $300 interest and subtracting $600 in total payments to obtain a balance of $9,700. In fact, if $300 were actually collected the interest rate would not be 6% compounded semiannually but approximately 6.22% compounded semiannually. This would then contravene the mortgage agreement.

Simple vs. Compound Interest

Question: On a $10,000 loan at 7% compounded semiannually and payable in monthly payments of $100, principal plus interest, I calculate the interest of the first payment to be $58.33. Your figure is $57.50. Please explain the difference.

Answer: When you calculated the interest payment, you probably used a simple interest calculation. If you did this, you are assuming, incorrectly, that interest is compounded monthly. The computation schedules are based on the assumption that interest is compounded as stated, that is, semiannually. Examine the schedules below.

Loan $10,000 Rate 7% Compounded Monthly Payments $100 Payable Monthly

Simple Interest

Payment Number	Interest Payment	Principal Payment	Balance of Loan
1	$58.33	$41.67	$9958.33
2	58.09	41.91	9916.42
3	57.85	42.15	9874.27
4	57.60	42.40	9831.87

Loan $10,000 Rate 7% Compounded Semiannually Payment $100 Payable Monthly

Compound Interest

Payment Number	Interest Payment	Principal Payment	Balance of Loan
1	57.50	42.50	9957.50
2	57.26	42.74	9914.76
3	57.01	42.99	9871.77
4	56.76	43.24	9828.53

Examine your schedule carefully. It should correspond to the lender's figures. Make certain he has a copy of the schedule (an example is shown on page 97).

Note that:

1. The basic amounts should correspond exactly to your mortgage terms.

2. Compounding should be identical to the statement of interest in your mortgage: e.g. 9% per annum calculated (compounded) *semiannually* not in advance.

3. The first payment is recorded and made on the proper date.

4. If the compounding is semiannual, the amount of interest on the first payment is *less than* one-twelfth of $25,000 times the annual interest rate. The lender and borrower should both be aware of this: $184.08 is less than $25,000 × 9% ÷ 12 = $187.50.

5. Each payment and exact current balance can be easily kept track of by checking off each date as the payment is made.

6. The interest portion plus the principal portion will add up to the total payment amount.

7. The interest on each subsequent payment is slightly less than the interest on the previous pay-

The Computerized Schedule
(Courtesy CSC, P.O. Box 400, Willowdale, Ont.)

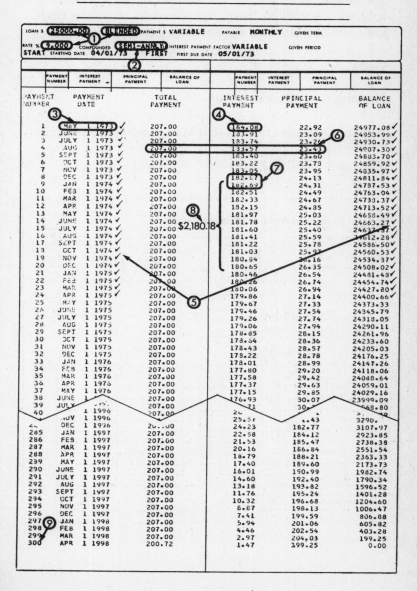

LOAN $ 25000.00 BLENDED PAYMENT $ VARIABLE PAYABLE MONTHLY GIVEN TERM

RATE % 9.000 COMPOUNDED SEMI-ANN.Y. INTEREST PAYMENT FACTOR VARIABLE GIVEN PERIOD

START STARTING DATE 04/01/73 FIRST FIRST DUE DATE 05/01/73

PAYMENT NUMBER	PAYMENT DATE	TOTAL PAYMENT	INTEREST PAYMENT	PRINCIPAL PAYMENT	BALANCE OF LOAN
1	MAY 1 1973	207.00	164.08	22.92	24977.08
2	JUNE 1 1973	207.00	183.91	23.09	24953.99
3	JULY 1 1973	207.00	183.74	23.26	24930.73
4	AUG 1 1973	207.00	183.57	23.43	24907.30
5	SEPT 1 1973	207.00	183.40	23.60	24883.70
6	OCT 1 1973	207.00	183.22	23.78	24859.92
7	NOV 1 1973	207.00	183.05	23.95	24835.97
8	DEC 1 1973	207.00	182.87	24.13	24811.84
9	JAN 1 1974	207.00	182.69	24.31	24787.53
10	FEB 1 1974	207.00	182.51	24.49	24763.04
11	MAR 1 1974	207.00	182.33	24.67	24738.37
12	APR 1 1974	207.00	182.15	24.85	24713.52
13	MAY 1 1974	207.00	181.97	25.03	24688.49
14	JUNE 1 1974	207.00	181.78	25.22	24663.27
15	JULY 1 1974	207.00	181.60	25.40	24637.87
16	AUG 1 1974	207.00	181.41	25.59	24612.28
17	SEPT 1 1974	207.00	181.22	25.78	24586.50
18	OCT 1 1974	207.00	181.03	25.97	24560.53
19	NOV 1 1974	207.00	180.84	26.16	24534.37
20	DEC 1 1974	207.00	180.65	26.35	24508.02
21	JAN 1 1975	207.00	180.46	26.54	24481.48
22	FEB 1 1975	207.00	180.26	26.74	24454.74
23	MAR 1 1975	207.00	180.06	26.94	24427.80
24	APR 1 1975	207.00	179.86	27.14	24400.66
25	MAY 1 1975	207.00	179.67	27.33	24373.33
26	JUNE 1 1975	207.00	179.46	27.54	24345.79
27	JULY 1 1975	207.00	179.26	27.74	24318.05
28	AUG 1 1975	207.00	179.06	27.94	24290.11
29	SEPT 1 1975	207.00	178.85	28.15	24261.96
30	OCT 1 1975	207.00	178.64	28.36	24233.60
31	NOV 1 1975	207.00	178.43	28.57	24205.03
32	DEC 1 1975	207.00	178.22	28.78	24176.25
33	JAN 1 1976	207.00	178.01	28.99	24147.26
34	FEB 1 1976	207.00	177.80	29.20	24118.06
35	MAR 1 1976	207.00	177.58	29.42	24088.64
36	APR 1 1976	207.00	177.37	29.63	24059.01
37	MAY 1 1976	207.00	177.15	29.85	24029.16
38	JUNE 1 1976	207.00	176.93	30.07	23999.09
39	JULY 1 ...	207.00	176.71	30...	23...
40	... 1 1996	207.00	20...	25.5?	...668.80
2..	NOV 1 1996	...	25.57	..43	3290..
2..	DEC 1 1996	20...00	24.23	182.77	3107.97
285	JAN 1 1997	207.00	22.98	184.12	2923.85
286	FEB 1 1997	207.00	21.53	185.47	2738.38
287	MAR 1 1997	207.00	20.16	186.84	2551.54
288	APR 1 1997	207.00	18.79	188.21	2363.33
289	MAY 1 1997	207.00	17.40	189.60	2173.73
290	JUNE 1 1997	207.00	16.01	190.99	1982.74
291	JULY 1 1997	207.00	14.60	192.40	1790.34
292	AUG 1 1997	207.00	13.18	193.82	1596.52
293	SEPT 1 1997	207.00	11.76	195.24	1401.28
294	OCT 1 1997	207.00	10.32	196.68	1204.60
295	NOV 1 1997	207.00	8.87	198.13	1006.47
296	DEC 1 1997	207.00	7.41	199.59	806.88
297	JAN 1 1998	207.00	5.94	201.06	605.82
298	FEB 1 1998	207.00	4.46	202.54	403.28
299	MAR 1 1998	207.00	2.97	204.03	199.25
300	APR 1 1998	200.72	1.47	199.25	0.00

$2,180.18

ment. Verify that this occurs not just once each half year but for every payment.

8. The interest accumulated over a calendar year is mandatory information for lenders who must declare interest as income. Send the schedule (copy) in with your income tax as a supporting document.

9. Verify that the mortgage pays out in twenty-five years.

Obtaining the Schedule

Here is a sample of how to fill in a schedule order form:

(Courtesy CSC P.O. Box 400, Willowdale, Ont.)

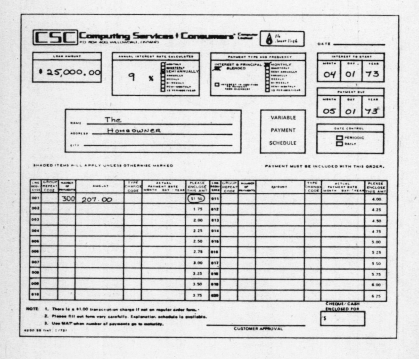

State the:

1. Loan amount.

2. Annual interest rate and compounding.

3. Blended payments (interest and principal included in one payment) *or* fixed principal payments only, with interest in addition (non-blended).

4. Date that interest is to be calculated from (usually the mortgage closing date).

5. Date the first payment is due.

6. Date control; *periodic* means that payments are made on a regular day each month.

7. Number of payments until the mortgage is paid off.

8. The amount of each payment.

Other Computerized Schedule Services

There are many variations of the mortgage repayment schedule. Some examples and their uses are:

1. The Variable Payment Schedule (page 97) can be used for many other situations. It will handle payments that change, extra lump sum payments, tax payments (as minus amounts), investment situations, missed payments, payments made on different dates and payments that are not large enough to cover the interest. The payment amount and payment date can be listed for each individual transaction.

2. The Regular Mortgage Repayment Schedule is similar to the above except that it does not include dates or any variations.

3. The Level-Balance Schedule calculates interest on a fixed balance over six months. The interest amount decreases only once every six months. It has the effect of not crediting the principal portion of each payment until six months have elapsed.

4. The Wraparound Schedule is used by a borrower to secure additional funds. The borrower gives a third party a mortgage blanketing an existing mortgage. The new lender covenants to be responsible to maintain the existing mortgage payments, lends the borrower the additional funds (secured by a mortgage) and the borrower then makes his mortgage payment to the new mortgagee.

5. Yield Calculations: Lenders buy and sell mortgages between themselves just as goods are bought and sold. The purchaser will often want to discount the mortgage so as to yield a higher rate of interest.

6. Interest Calculations: A series of sixteen special calculations are available. Want to find an effective interest rate? Convert an *add-on advance* rate to *not-in-advance*? Calculate a present worth on a loan amount? Evaluate a fund accumulation?

7. Table Services: A number of tables are available for the finance business. Examples are small loans consumer tables for instalment financing and conversion tables for metric, mensuration, payroll, and tax conversions.

The Computer Tells You

Some of the things that these schedules and calculations will show you are very interesting. For example, if you had arranged a $25,000 mortgage, 25 year, at 9% compounded twice yearly with a blended payment of $207 per month you could:

1. Increase your monthly payment:
   (i) $ 5 more to $212 saves $ 3,500 in interest.
   (ii) $10 more to $217 saves $ 6,300 in interest.
   (iii) $20 more to $227 saves $10,500 in interest.
   (iv) $50 more to $257 saves $17,900 in interest.

2. Prepay with borrowed money: Make extra anniversary payments with borrowed money at a higher rate, say 10%. Pay this loan back over a year.

   (i) $ 500 borrowed each year at 10% saves $15,300

   (ii) $1,000 borrowed each year at 10% saves $20,900

3. Pay fixed principal interest: Divide the $25,000.00 into equal principal amounts of $83.33 per month over 25 years. You pay more on the first payments and less thereafter. You save $9,300.00.

4. Avoid paying "simple interest." Dividing by twelve means total interest repaid is $40,444 rather than $37,093 (if the rate is compounded semi-annually). You save $3,300.

5. Avoid the "level-balance" technique: The borrower pays $41,649 rather than $37,093. You save $4,500.

6. Avoid extending the amortization period. A 1% interest rate raise to 10% after 5 years with the payment remaining at $207 per month means you pay $14,000 more than the original $37,093 in interest.

7. Did you know that $85 per month invested at 1% per month for 40 years makes you a millionaire?

All calculations above are illustrations only. Specific calculations are to be interpreted in accordance with the terms of the particular mortgage document. The calculations do not include adjustments for taxes, inflation and/or interest earned on alternative investments.

For further information on the foregoing, and to obtain your tailor-made mortgage repayment schedules, write:

     CSC Amortization Department,
     P.O. Box 400, Willowdale, Ont.

21
Averaging the Interest Rate

If you wish to know what your annual rate of interest is on a combination of mortgages, here is how to do it:

Take the percent of each mortgage to the total debt (of 100%) and multiply by its rate of interest:

Example		Principal Amount
1st mortgage:	8%	$16,000
2nd mortgage:	14%	4,000
Total mortgage debt:		$20,000

$$\frac{16,000}{20,000} \times \frac{100}{1} = 80\% \times 8\% = 6.4\%$$

$$\frac{4,000}{20,000} \times \frac{100}{1} = 20\% \times 14\% = 2.8\%$$

Total: 100% (average) 9.2%

Example		Principal Amount
1st mortgage:	8.25%	$12,544
2nd mortgage:	10.50%	3,724
3rd mortgage:	13.00%	3,332
Total mortgage debt:		$19,600

$$\frac{12{,}544}{19{,}600} \times \frac{100}{1} = 64\% \times 8.25\% = 5.280\%$$

$$\frac{3{,}724}{19{,}600} \times \frac{100}{1} = 19\% \times 10.50\% = 1.995\%$$

$$\frac{3{,}332}{19{,}600} \times \frac{100}{1} = 17\% \times 13.00\% = 2.210\%$$

Total: 100% (average) 9.485%

Here is another way to do it. Follow the figures I have given you in the second example, and round out the interest on an annual basis:

	Principal	Interest
1st mortgage:	$12,544 @ 8.25%	$1,034.88
2nd mortgage:	3,724 @ 10.50%	391.12
3rd mortgage:	3,332 @ 13.00%	433.16
	$19,600	$1,859.16

Now, just divide the interest by the principal and multiply by one hundred:

$$\frac{1{,}859.16}{19{,}600.00} \times \frac{100}{1} = 9.485\%$$

Same thing, see?

22
Foreclosure

Years ago, it was the accepted practice for lenders to recover loans by way of a writ of foreclosure.

Here were the basic rules in Ontario:

The lender's lawyer, having a good sense of propriety, sent a letter to the borrower advising him that if late payments were not brought up to date forthwith, further legal action would be necessary, and costly.

If the borrower did nothing about it, a writ of foreclosure was served by a sheriff's officer, which made the matter very serious business. Some lawyers, of course — and I suspect through nothing else but greed — didn't bother with a warning letter.

They just charged ahead with the writ, tacking hundreds of dollars onto it for their trouble.

If the borrower did not seek legal advice, and ignored the writ, the lender could proceed to gain title to the property and the matter would be at an end.

Of course, all subsequent encumbrances would be also served, having the opportunity to pay off the plaintiff mortgagee and own the mortgage.

When the lender obtained a final order of foreclosure, the borrower forfeited all equity he had in the property. This was the sad part. However, if the lender later sold the property, and didn't get enough to cover his mortgage loan, it was too bad for him.

There were three basic things a borrower could do about a writ of foreclosure:

- He could bring arrears up to date within the time specified by the writ, pay the lender's legal fees, and carry on making payments under the mortgage.
- He could pay into court $150 and ask that the property be sold by the sheriff's office. After the sale — and after paying for its cost, the mortgage debt, and everybody having liens against the property — the borrower would be paid any money left over.

    This could prevent him from losing his equity in the property. But if there was a shortage in the mortgage account, he could be sued.
- He could file a request to redeem the mortgaged property. This would give him a period of six months, after taking of the account of the amount due the lender, in which to get the money to settle the matter.

Sometimes the legal business of figuring out precisely how much was owing (taking of the account) could delay matters for a couple of months, which meant the borrower had eight months on his side.

Despite the advantage of an occasional property gain by foreclosure, the long, drawn-out business was a drag for most lenders, especially financial institutions which just wanted the debt repaid. So it became more popular and quicker to proceed by notice under a power of sale.

This cleans the matter up in a matter of weeks, instead of months. After the sale, any money left after paying everybody off is given to the borrower, the one who lost the property.

But if the sale doesn't produce enough to pay off the lender and his lawyer, the borrower will be sued for the balance.

Now — and read this carefully — the period of time allowed to redeem property in a foreclosure action has been reduced from six months to *60 days*.

I believe some private lenders will view this as an invitation to return to foreclosures and the opportunity of getting something for nothing; the borrower's equity.

If you are a borrower on shaky ground, don't lose your lawyer's phone number.

And another thing, the ante for a borrower asking for a judicial sale is now $250.

23
The Power of Sale

In Ontario, nothing can cause a homeowner more grief than receiving a notice from his mortgagee that it is exercising its right under the "power of sale" provision in the mortgage deed.

There is a lot of this going on, and with massive unemployment it will get worse. Aside from shyster lenders and others who have no patience with delinquent borrowers, here is what you may expect from conventional mortgagees such as banks and trust companies when your mortgage is in arrears.

You will receive one or two letters from your lender demanding that arrears be brought up to date. If you ignore them, you will receive an initial letter from the lender's solicitor, reminding you about your overdue payments, along with a demand for payment plus a fee for his services in writing the letter.

Ignore this, and you get another letter from the same solicitor demanding more money for his services, plus mortgage arrears, and a warning about the lender selling your home to satisfy the debt.

Ignore this and you will receive a notice under a power of sale, which will say that the entire amount of the mortgage principal plus interest arrears, plus a whopping legal fee must be paid by a date a couple of days beyond 35 days of receipt of the registered notice.

You will receive it, and so will your spouse and any party holding judgment executions against you. It won't do any good to refuse the registered notice, because the law says that when it was placed in the hands of the post office it was "delivered", whether you accepted it or not.

Your initial reaction will be that if you can't pay the arrears, how do they expect you to pay the whole thing? What the notice doesn't say is that if the mortgage term has not reached its end, usually you don't have to.

But you must make the late payments, and pay the lawyer's charges, which will be added to your mortgage debt.

When you receive the notice, do not delay or procrastinate in doing something about it. If you ignore it all, and the time limit expires, you will receive a notice to vacate your home within a few days; if you ignore this, you will be evicted by the sheriff. And your home will be sold.

It will not be given away as distress merchandise, but on the other hand your mortgagee will be under no obligation to wait for a top market price.

Such short notices will provide extreme hardships because even if you have a chance to immediately rent a house, you will have to put up the first and last month's rent which will probably be at least fifteen hundred dollars. Even an apartment means laying out about one thousand.

Then you will have moving expenses to pay, plus all the disruptions of moving on short notice. And it will be short, because the lender is not in any mood to do you any favors at this stage of the game.

If you make part payment to a bank branch thinking that this will delay the fatal day by causing the lender to go around again, don't count on it. You will receive a letter acknowledging the payment, but subject to the lender's rights under the power of sale.

Other than raising money for your arrears, the only recourse you have is to sell your home. And this is where you especially need the broad shoulders of a good lawyer to intercede on your behalf.

Your home could be put on the market and sold before the power of sale notice is received, but have your lawyer call the lender and let it know what you are doing. This will show a bit of good faith, and you will probably receive a sympathetic hearing at this point.

If it is sold during the term of the sale notice, you will still have to bring the arrears up to date within the time limit. If the sale is a good, solid one with no conditions, your lawyer is a good man to look to for interim financing. He'll get the advanced money back out of the proceeds of the sale.

I cannot stress too strongly the importance of good legal counsel early in your misfortune.

Don't allow your family to be thrown out on the street.

The Lenders' Responsibilities

The lender (or mortgagee) who has paved the way to sell a house under his power-of-sale has certain responsibilities which should not be taken lightly.

He properly serves the borrower (or mortgagor) with his notice, which the borrower does nothing about. Then the lender has the homeowner evicted, leaving the lender with an empty house on his hands.

At this point, some lenders undoubtedly are of the opinion they can then sell the property for any price as long as it covers the mortgage debt and legal fees.

Fortunately, we have courts that take a dim view of

such behavior and have gone so far as to render sales
null and void made under such circumstances.

Large conventional lenders normally take the safe
route and do it properly, ensuring that the borrower
who is losing his property at least gets a fair shake out
of his misfortune. But not always, it seems.

The Bank of Nova Scotia, as lender and mortgagee,
had a sale criticized and was penalized by a court
because the property was sold too cheaply. Whether
this was the active fault of the bank is not for me to
say, but here is what happened:

The bank sold a property under power-of-sale for
$45,000. The court found the value of the property was
about $65,000 and decided it had been sold too
cheaply.

The bank was held responsible for selling in a negli-
gent and careless fashion and had to compensate the
former owner of the property for this.

It was observed that the bank didn't put forth
enough effort in the sale and said the property should
have received wide exposure by placing it on multiple-
listing, a service provided by a real estate board.

While judges have on more than one occasion said a
lender is not a trustee in the power-of-sale, and can
give preference to its own interests, they have also
said the lender must act in good faith and take reasonable precaution in obtaining the true-market value of
the property at the time it wishes to sell it.

One court stated that the prime duty of such a lender
is to act *bona fide* in exercising the power of sale. It
went on to list further duties of the lender:

• To try to realize the fair value of the property.
• To deduct only reasonable expenses of sale from the
  proceeds.

- To consider the interests of the borrower as well as the lender's own interests.
- Not to conduct the sale in bad faith.

It would therefore be prudent for a lender to first have the property properly appraised. The cost of this, of course, would come off the top in the accounting to the borrower.

Next, have the property listed on a multiple-listing service, which would give it wide exposure.

These two basic steps would show good faith to all and the lender could not be criticized for attempting to take advantage of a hapless borrower by sacrificing the property in order to gain his own quick ends.

The broker listing the property should certainly have his "for sale" sign on the front lawn and the lender should ensure the broker earns his money by doing a bit of advertising also.

A major problem in obtaining a reasonable market price is that many people think power-of-sale means nothing but bargains. Make a lowball offer. Steal something!

A responsible lender will not be impressed by such people and with reasonable effort on the part of his broker, a decent market price will be realized.

The one who lost the property receives what's left after everything is paid off so it would be in his own best interests to ask his lawyer to do what he can to ensure that he is getting treated fairly.

24
The Oklahoma Offer

One of the meanest financial flim-flams devised and used by money-grabbers is the "Oklahoma Offer." It is slick, professional and, to the untrained eye, hard to spot. It enables one to purchase property with nothing down and make a substantial and immediate cash profit.

Unfortunately, it leaves a vendor (property seller) stuck with a mortgage, most of which is not worth the paper it is written on. If you are selling property, watch for it. Here is an example of how it works.

The following are briefly the financial contents of an offer to purchase property:

1. Purchase Price: $47,000
2. Deposit with Offer: $ 2,000
3. Purchaser agrees to pay vendor $30,000 on closing.
4. Vendor agrees to hold second mortgage for $15,000.
5. Purchaser agrees to arrange, at his own expense, a first mortgage of not less than $30,000.

The innocent vendor adds it up:

Deposit:	$ 2,000
Cash:	30,000
Mortgage:	15,000
Total:	$47,000

If the offer is accepted, the purchaser can go to work and arrange a first mortgage of not $30,000 but $40,000. Remember, it was agreed that the first mortgage will be *not less than $30,000.*

Out of this $40,000 first mortgage, the purchaser will pay the vendor the agreed $30,000, give himself $2,000 to get back the deposit, and put $8,000 profit in his pocket.

Proof?

First Mortgage:	$40,000
Second Mortgage:	15,000
	$55,000
Purchase Price:	47,000
Profit to buyer:	$ 8,000

The vendor, having agreed to hold a second mortgage of $15,000, is now in the unenviable position of having $8,000 of the $15,000 mortgage *exceed* the purchase price of the property.

If the purchaser is a corporate shell with no assets, it could then walk away with the $8,000 profit and forget the property.

If the vendor (now the second mortgagee) ended up owning the property again, he would owe $40,000 to a first mortgagee. Here is the spot he would be in:

Property worth	$47,000
Owing	40,000
Equity worth	7,000
Cash received	32,000
	$39,000
Selling price:	47,000
Net loss to vendor:	($ 8,000)

(plus headaches and legal fees)

What this means, of course, is that it will cost the vendor (mortgagee) $8,000 out of his own pocket to regain possession of the property.

This money-making scheme is triggered by a clause in the agreement that will allow the purchaser (mortgagor) to increase the principal amount of the first mortgage "without necessarily applying the increase to reduce the principal amount of the second mortgage," which allows the purchaser to arrange and secure the $40,000 mortgage.

If questioned on this nocuous point, a glib person will say something to the effect that money obtained from such an increase will be required to improve the property, resulting in greater security for the second mortgagee (vendor). Which is hogwash! Watch it!

Also, the purchaser may ask to assign the agreement to a third, unnamed party. This will release the purchaser from his covenant, and the assignee could be a corporate shell with no assets.

And, in *any* agreement of purchase and sale, here are two warnings signs. Be careful about accepting an offer from a buyer who shows the words "in trust" after his name. "In trust" could be a corporate shell with no money and, when the time comes to close, it would be useless to attempt to force a closing legally if the purchaser decided not to close. It is tantamount to giving the purchaser an option on the property. Therefore, a serious consideration must be the amount of the deposit made with the offer and the length of time to close the sale. If the purchaser defaults, the vendor could retain the deposit money, which should be an amount considered to be fair compensation for the length of time the property was tied up . . .

When selling an older property, be careful as well about agreeing to warrant that there will be no municipal or other legal work orders registered against the property on the date of closing. A sharp purchaser, under such an agreement, could have the property inspected by municipal fire and building departments resulting in unheard of orders to repair and/or improve the property. The vendor would be stuck with the bill. Agree only to there being no work orders registered against the property on the date of acceptance of the agreement.

Caveat emptor? Let the buyer beware? Let the *seller* beware!

25
The Existing Mortgage

This mortgage is already registered against the property. Without reference to interest rates, it is the cheapest way to get a mortgage.

When purchasing property that already has a mortgage registered against it, which the buyer would like to use in financing the purchase, a part of the purchase agreement would say something like "the purchaser agrees to assume an existing first mortgage now registered against the property" with the details of the mortgage following this statement.

Well, what is the buyer really saying when he "agrees to assume" the mortgage? All he is really saying to the vendor is that he will maintain the mortgage payments without the permission of the mortgagee!

The vendor (or a previous owner) is the one who signed the mortgage deed and has the covenant and responsibility to repay the debt. The covenantor is not released of his obligation simply because he transfers his property equity to someone else.

So the buyer assumes the mortgage, takes possession of the property and continues making the payments required by the mortgage. As long as the payments are received in time, the mortgagee is happy and not the slightest bit concerned about the new guy.

When one buys a property and assumes an existing mortgage(s) consider the financial and other advantages:

(a) no mortgage application
(b) no credit check (very seldom)
(c) no waiting
(d) no mortgage appraisal fee
(e) no arranging fees
(f) no legal fees

It can save a buyer hundreds of dollars and, when the term expires, the buyer who is paying the mortgagee on time will have an excellent chance of obtaining an immediate renewal of the loan, providing it was originally obtained from a conventional source. Private lenders often do not wish to renew mortgage loans.

A buyer, especially one who is in no particular hurry, would be well advised to restrict his house hunting to properties that have mortgages already registered against them that would suit him. If one finds a property with an acceptable mortgage against it, but it falls short of loan requirements, study the availability of secondary financing and then average the interest rate in the total mortgage packages as outlined in Chapter 21. But if this route is taken, ensure that the *total* costs of the secondary financing are clearly understood.

The best and cheapest way to obtain secondary financing is covered in the following chapter, where the vendor lends a helping hand.

A point to remember is to read the actual mortgage deed if you intend to assume a mortgage. Some deeds have a non-transfer clause in them which means that if the secured property is sold, the mortgage must be paid off and, of course, if this is the case, you can just forget it and look for another one.

26
The Purchase Mortgage

Who says it is hard to borrow money?

A man with a horrible credit record would have difficulty floating a loan at his bank for a few hundred dollars, but the same man can borrow as much as *fifty thousand dollars* or more quite easily when buying a home.

How? Why, he simply borrows it from the one selling him the home. No credit check (or at least very seldom), no waiting for results of a mortgage application, instant approval of the loan, no problems. How about that?

It is the purchase mortgage, the mortgage held by the one selling the property. If one is looking for a top deal in a mortgage, here is where it is really possible.

When looking through the listing files of a real estate broker, this financing will be indicated on the listing by the notation "V.T.B." (Vendor Take Back) usually followed by "at current rates" which, of course, refers to the current market interest rates. What usually happens though, is that the buyer will make his offer to the vendor with the interest rate shown as lower than market rates and often he will get the deal.

There are two basic reasons for a vendor to agree to lend the buyer the money secured by the mortgage.

(a) It is considered to be a good investment. A mortgage on property that is security familiar to the vendor, which produces a higher yield than other usual investments.

(b) It makes the property very saleable because of the financing available to the buyer.

The purchase mortgage does not necessarily have to be one first mortgage. The majority of purchase mortgages are second mortgages, which are created after:

(a) The buyer assumes an existing first mortgage.

(b) The buyer arranges a new first mortgage, *or* a vendor might agree to hold two mortgages, a first and a second, the larger the first mortgage and the smaller the second. The reasons would be:

 (i) Two separate mortgage deeds create two separate securities.

(ii) The vendor, holding the two mortgages, could perhaps give one to a relative, or use them as security in borrowing money on two separate occasions. Some people follow the old adage "don't put all your eggs in one basket".

Any way one looks at it, a property offered with the vendor helping with the financing can be a sweet deal.

In taking advantage of this financing, ensure that there is an "open" privilege clause inserted in the mortgage deed which will enable the borrower to repay any part or all of the outstanding principal balance at any time (or on any payment date) without notice or bonus.

27
Pros and Cons of the Purchase Mortgage

Would you lend a stranger $50,000 cash?

It is done every day by people selling their homes and accepting a mortgage from a buyer as part of the purchase price. Here are some advantages and disadvantages to this, and sensible guidelines to follow:

The advantages are:

- The security for the loan is land, which is permanent. It won't go away. Anytime you need reassurance that your loan is secure, just go and take a look. Still there.
- Furthermore, it is security that is familiar to you: Your own home. If the borrower goes into serious default, you could end up with the security back in your own hands through foreclosure. Not a nice thought, but after all it is your money.
- The interest you will receive on the loan will be more than you can get from current bank interest. Mortgages pay more than a bank can afford to pay you.

  When lending the money, you can make the loan renewable on an annual basis if you wish, and adjust the interest rate to current market rates. That way you can keep ahead of what banks will pay.

  However, remember that trying to predict future

rates is a futile exercise. If rates go down, you lose. If they go up, you win. If you accept a fixed rate for a number of years at least you can budget with a known income.

- Offering to accept a mortgage makes it attractive for a buyer, because he knows where he can get instant financing and save all the legal and other charges of arranging a third party mortgage. It can also result in a higher selling price of your home because of this.

The disadvantages are:
- Your money is tied up in a security that, although very sound, will probably have to be sold at a discount if you need the cash.

   If you wish to keep the mortgage, you will not necessarily be able to borrow the full face value of it if such a need arises.
- The borrower, being an individual, is naturally a poorer risk for the loan than a bank would be. There is always the danger of having problems receiving payments on time, or worse, not receiving them at all. You can get your money back all right, but with such problems it takes time.

My sensible guidelines are:
- Before lending a stranger a large sum of money you should run a credit check on him, and also see if there are any judgment executions registered against him.

   He might seem like the greatest guy in the world to you, but if he has a severe debt load it could create problems for you. Also, it would be a good idea to check his employment record and obtain references.
- The amount of the loan is most important. If you sell your property for about 10% down, I certainly would

not recommend holding a mortgage for the balance of the purchase price.

With the vagaries of a housing market, the 10% equity in the property could be eroded, leaving you with a mortgage of the entire market value of the property. If problems arose in repayment, it would be unlikely that you would recover your entire loan.

A safe limit in lending would be to ensure that your loan does not exceed 75% of the selling price. And if the buyer obtains first mortgage financing and asks you for secondary financing, ensure that the total amount of the first mortgage and the amount of your second mortgage does not exceed the 75%.

Of course, the buyer would be free to obtain further financing secured by other mortgages, but they would not affect the safety of your own mortgage seniority.

I shall never cease to be amazed at the almost casual way a seller will agree to hold a mortgage when accepting an offer. Take your time and think about it.

The Dangers of Low Downpayments

You think that because a first mortgage has a priority, there is nothing to worry about? Think again.

Recently a small house in a rural community sold for $26,000. One first mortgage of $21,000 was taken back by the seller.

The agreement said the balance of the purchase price would be paid by certified cheque.

Seems reasonable, but what happened was a disaster for the seller.

The accepted offer called for a deposit of $500 and here is where all the trouble really began.

Unknown to the seller, the buyer arranged to borrow $4,500 from a private source, which was secured by a second mortgage.

The seller was paid the $5,000 and received a first mortgage to secure the balance of the selling price.

Of course, a real estate commission and legal fees came out of this, which left the seller with about $3,000 cash.

The buyer didn't move into the house. It was immediately rented, with the rent going right into his pocket.

Not one payment was made on the seller's first mortgage or to the owner of the second mortgage.

Now, what have we got? A real mess, that's what.

The buyer disappeared, apparently turning up once a month to pick up the rent.

Oh, I know, there are all kinds of legal courses open to the lenders in those mortgage deeds, but who needs all that flak?

Both lenders handed their money over in good faith and all they can look forward to now are legal bills for straightening out the mess.

In any legal action to recover money in a mortgage, the borrower has the responsibility of paying the bills.

But if he hasn't got any money and is hard to find, all it will amount to is payment by a series of headaches, without the money. Kiss it goodbye.

The foregoing gives a seller and a lender several warning signs. Here are two of the better ones:

• Accepting a modest payment such as $500 as a deposit with an offer to buy your property could be a fatal mistake. It could mean the buyer is short of money.

   Some agents, when confronted by this thought, will tell the seller that the buyer has money "tied up" in stocks or bonds and it will take a few days to cash them in. Not to worry.

Oh yeah? If you hear this, tell your agent to remind the buyer money can be quickly raised by borrowing against the securities. Demand more money as a deposit, or at least more solid evidence of where it is coming from.

Of course, there is nothing to prevent the buyer from eventually raising the money by secondary financing.

In the example I have cited, the buyer never had any more than $500, so demanding more money would have cancelled the deal — and prevented a lot of grief.

- If you are asked to lend money through secondary mortgaging, take a good look at the arithmetic.

If there is going to be an owner's cash equity of just $500 after adding up the mortgage totals, forget it. Look at the problems that confronted the second mortgage lender in this deal!

The second mortgagee bought the first mortgage at a $3,000 discount.

The seller lost and the second mortgagee became first mortgagee.

28
CMHC and NHA Loans

CMHC Direct Loans

This type of loan is getting scarce. It is intended to make money available for borrowers in smaller communities, and in the country where conventional mortgage loans are not available.

The rate of interest in the loan will be the same as NHA loans obtained through banks etc. in larger centers, and the money comes directly from CMHC and not from the approved NHA lender.

If you are out in the sticks or in a small town, write Canada Mortgage and Housing Corporation, Ottawa, Ontario, and ask if such funds are currently available in your area.

NHA Loans

These are called NHA mortgages because they come under the concept of Canada's National Housing Act, administered by a Crown corporation called Canada Mortgage and Housing Corporation.

The money is borrowed from approved lenders of CMHC such as banks and trust companies. The interest rates are not set, but are normally within the current market ranges.

When a loan is approved by a bank, for example, the bank will send the money, through its lawyer, to the party entitled to it, such as one selling the borrower a house.

In addition to the principal amount of the loan, the borrower will agree to pay an insurance fee which may be added to the mortgage.

The bank also puts up the money for this insurance fee (which is loaned to the borrower) and sends it to CMHC which places the money in an insurance fund.

This mortgage insurance, paid by the borrower in favor of the lender, is to protect the lender in case of default by the borrower.

In addition to an annual principal repayment feature of a portion of the principal sum, NHA mortgages are "open" in three years, and may be paid off with a three months' interest penalty.

29
Different Types of Mortgages

The Conventional Mortgage

This mortgage is called conventional because it is the customary, prevalent and most commonly used method of obtaining a mortgage loan.

When an agreement to buy a house is made, a conditional clause is often inserted in the agreement giving the buyer about ten days to arrange a new mortgage. Immediately on acceptance of the purchase agreement by buyer and seller, the buyer makes application (usually through the suggestions of the real estate broker who made the sale) to a mortgage lender such as a bank, insurance, or trust company.

It is a sound move to follow the suggestion of a real estate or mortgage broker in making the application, because the broker is on top of the money market and knows not only where the best flow of money happens to be, but where he can get the fastest action in the application (which adds a little glue to the sale).

If the buyer is a person of means and one with an excellent credit rating, he could buy the property without the conditional clause simply because he would have no difficulty in obtaining financing. Vendors are more willing to sell without conditional clauses in the sales agreements.

It is quite common to have a 10% annual principal prepayment clause in today's conventional mortgage.

The Blanket Mortgage

The original concept of a blanket mortgage probably began with a house builder.

A builder obtains an agreement with a lending institution to cover (blanket) it financially in the construction of a multiple housing project. The original mortgage deed signed by the builder will cover the entire project, and as the construction of houses progresses, the borrower will be given loan advances to pay the bills.

Finally, when the houses reach the selling stage, a buyer for house number one will appear and sign an agreement to buy the first house from the builder, subject to credit approval.

The builder then marches the buyer down to the blanket mortgagee's office where a mortgage application is processed. If approved, the one house sold is taken off the covenant in the builder's blanket mortgage and a single mortgage for the house buyer's signature is prepared.

The builder and his lender proceed in this fashion until all the houses are sold, and the original blanket mortgage which covered the entire project is reduced to zero and discharged.

This is a very favourable method for large lenders to place funds, because they can do it in large chunks initially which will be reduced and spread over hundreds of individuals eventually. It makes for easier and faster accounting of the lenders' budgets because of the size of the initial mortgages.

The Umbrella Mortgage

When a borrower wishes to float a loan secured by a mortgage, the equity in the proposed realty to be used for security sometimes is not large enough to satisfy the lender.

If the borrower owned more than one parcel of realty, he could borrow against each parcel but this would normally require separate mortgage deeds.

So, sometimes the borrower will put up more than one parcel to secure the loan, and sign just one mortgage deed to cover all the parcels used for security.

The mortgage will be registered on title against each parcel so secured.

One mortgage. One payment. *Voilà*, the umbrella mortgage, which umbrellas more than one parcel.

A clause would probably be in the mortgage deed covering the eventuality that the borrower may wish to sell one or more of the secured parcels of property. This clause would stipulate the principal reduction and possible penalty required if carried out.

The Wraparound Mortgage

A type of mortgage (commonly called a blanket) that is gaining popularity in Canada is a wraparound mortgage. This mortgage "blankets" an existing mortgage.

With no relation to current mortgage rates, and based on simple interest calculations, the following will illustrate the mechanics of this type of mortgage.

Assume you wish to buy a house for $50,000. The realty has an 8% mortgage registered against it with an outstanding principal balance of $25,000. You have $12,000, which of course is $13,000 short of the required cash needed to buy the property. The existing mortgagee (lender) won't increase the first mortgage. You shop around and discover that the going rate for secondary financing is 13%, which seems a little stiff. The vendor won't help.

Now, this is where the blanket mortgage lender may

enter the picture. He proposes that you put up your $12,000, and he will lend you sufficient funds to enable you to buy your home — namely $38,000 at 11%.

This is where a sharp pencil comes in handy. If the current going rate of first mortgage financing is 10%, this offer is just 1% higher. Simple arithmetic will tell you that just an extra $380 a year on $38,000 will enable you to buy the house, with the realization that the house will undoubtedly go up in value by a lot more than $380 a year!

Well, what about the $25,000 balance on the existing mortgage that is registered against the realty? The blanket lender will agree to be responsible for keeping up the payments on the existing mortgage, and will warrant it by making this promise a covenant in the mortgage deed you sign.

What the lender is doing is:

1. Agreeing to accept a second mortgage from you for $38,000 at 11%.
2. Registering the mortgage behind the existing first mortgage with the $25,000 balance and agreeing to maintain its payments.

With the results that:

1. He is lending you $13,000 at 11%.
2. He is allowing you to pay him 11% on $25,000, which he in turn repays at 8% (the rate on the registered first mortgage).
3. He could invest his $13,000 at 13% but he sacrifices 2% on $13,000 to pick up 3% on $25,000:

3% on $25,000:	$750
Less 2% on $13,000:	260
His annual gain:	$490

This is equal to the lender receiving 16¾% on his loan to you of $13,000.

When the $38,000 second mortgage is registered against the title to your realty, the existing $25,000 mortgage also remains, which means that $63,000 will be the registered debt against the land. However, the second mortgagee agrees to maintain the payments on the $25,000 portion of the debt.

The second mortgage will not have a term that will be longer than the remaining number of years in the term of the first mortgage. If, for example, the first mortgage had seven years remaining, the second mortgage would have a term of perhaps five years. Here is what happens at the end of the five years when the second mortgage becomes due.

Remember, the second mortgagee has invested $13,000 cash so the mortgagor (borrower) will pay him 13/38 of the principal amount of the mortgage, less all principal reductions, *plus* the principal sum which the second mortgagee has paid off the registered 8% first mortgage.

The mortgagor would then proceed to continue payments on the 8% first mortgage.

At this point, of course, the borrower would have to provide the funds to pay the second mortgagee, which would come from the borrower's own pocket, secondary financing, or a possible increase in the first mortgage.

Not bad for the lender, but what about you, the borrower? You were offered $13,000 at 13%. If you agree to this, here is your picture:

11% on $38,000		$4,180
8% on 25,000	$2,000	
13% on 13,000	1,690	3,690
Your annual gain:		$ 490

Which is exactly the gain the blanket lender was looking forward to . . .

Here is what you will actually pay for *all* your mortgaging if you go for the 13% second mortgage:

$$\frac{25,000}{38,000} \text{ x } \frac{100}{1} = 65.789\% \text{ x } 8\% = 5.26312\%$$

$$\frac{13,000}{38,000} \text{ x } \frac{100}{1} = 34.210\% \text{ x } 13\% = 4.44730\%$$

Average Interest Rate on $38,000: 9.71042%

Paying 9.7% is better than paying 11%.

What the lender must consider, of course, is the amount of principal he will be paying off the existing first mortgage with each payment. When this principal is paid, the lender can earn no interest on it until his own loan reaches maturity, at which time this principal will be recaptured and put to work.

If a blanket mortgage becomes available to you, use the above method of calculating, substituting your own figures, to determine if it would be advantageous.

The Piggyback Mortgage

Here's an example. A homeowner has a first mortgage registered against his property. He wants to borrow some money so he gets it from a private source and signs a mortgage deed that is registered as a second mortgage.

In this deed, there will be a clause requiring the mortgagor to do one of the following:

1. Provide the mortgagee in the second mortgage with monthly payments made payable to the first

mortgagee, which the second mortgage will post immediately to the first mortgagee.

2. Provide the mortgagee in the second mortgage with proof positive that the monthly payment on the first mortgage has been made. It will require that the proof be supplied within a specified period of time.

In other words, the second mortgagee is constantly on the borrower's back to ensure that the senior mortgage is always in good standing.

Piggyback!

The Leasehold Mortgage

Not all building owners own the land on which the building stands. The owners of some very large buildings in Canada lease the land under the buildings, which is called leasehold property. Leasehold property creates a leasehold mortgage.

Before a builder signs a ground lease, he will have an irrevocable mortgage commitment for his building. The mortgage requires an assignment of the ground lease, or sublease, and the terms of the ground lease will be satisfactory to the mortgagee, or there is no lease.

The principal sum of a leasehold mortgage is understandably less than it would be if the mortgagor owned the land.

If the mortgagee takes his mortgage under assignment of the lease, a situation is established between the lessor and mortgagee whereby the mortgagee becomes responsible for the terms of the lease, including that of paying the ground rent. The mortgagee would be liable for all breaches of covenant that might occur.

Under a sublease arrangement, the requirement

would be that the mortgagor would hold the last day of the term of the lease in trust for the mortgagee, in order to allow the mortgagee to control the last day and thereby control the renewable term. This is necessary, because although the mortgage term is usually of shorter duration than that of the lease, it could be possible for the mortgagee to have not received his final payments by the end of the term.

A leasehold mortgagee will most certainly protect himself fully to ensure that there is no termination of the ground lease, and will therefore have an agreement with the lessor to allow the mortgagee time to remedy any default on the part of the lessee.

The mortgage will contain a clause stipulating that a default by the mortgagor under the terms of the ground lease will automatically become a default under the mortgage.

The leasehold mortgage will require that the lessee pays the ground rent to the mortgagee, who in turn will pay it to the lessor, or require the lessee/mortgagor to produce receipts promptly.

This will answer the question: "Which has priority, the ground rent or the mortgage payment?"

Variable rate mortgage

Let's look at how a "variable rate" mortgage works. To simplify this, no principal payments will be made in the example — just interest. The mortgage limit will be 70% of the mortgage appraisal of the property. A real estate agent may say your property has a reasonable market value of $150,000, but the appraiser working for the mortgage lender may not agree.

If the mortgage appraiser says $140,000, then the borrowing limit will be 70% of that, or $98,000.

Conventional lenders usually go as high as 75% without resorting to mortgage insurance, which would bring the lending limit on this property to $105,000. The reason for the lower ratio will become apparent as you read on.

- The term can be as long as five years.
- The rate of interest in the mortgage will be the bank's prime lending rate, which is lower than market mortgage rates.
- The interest will be compounded monthly, and payable monthly. This simply means that if the prime rate in the mortgage is 12% a year, the borrower pays 1% a month. Just divide the contracted annual rate by 12.
- The mortgage can be paid off any time with a reasonable penalty. Now it gets interesting . . .

The bank prime rate will be adjusted once a month in the mortgage deed. If it goes up 1% in a monthly adjustment, a 12% loan becomes 13%. However, the payment remains the same.

How's that again? If the interest rate goes up, how can the monthly payment remain the same? Here's how it works:

Take the above figures. The borrower makes a monthly payment of 1% of the $98,000 ($980). When the rate goes to 13%, it would normally mean paying 1/12 of 13% of the $98,000 — or $1,061.66. but the payment stays at $980, leaving a shortage of $81.66.

This $81.66 is added to the mortgage debt, and now it is $98,081.66. In month two, the payment stays at $980 — and if the prime rate is still 13%, there will be another shortage. This time the payment will be short by $82.55, which is added to the debt.

Now, if the prime rate stays above the original contracted prime rate, the debt becomes larger each month. If it should get as high as 75% of the property value, then everybody takes another look at the loan, and one of two things will happen.

The property will be appraised again. If the appraisal indicates a higher figure, everybody just carries on, because the new appraisal will bring the loan ratio down to less than 75% of value.

But if the appraisal remains the same, the difference in each monthly payment — instead of being added to the loan principal — will be paid each month by the borrower and there will be no more increase in the loan amount.

Okay, so what happens if the prime rate goes below the original contracted rate? Well, the borrower makes the same $980 monthly payment, but now will have credit in his mortgage account.

He doesn't knock this off his payment or get a cash refund. It is taken off the outstanding principal amount of the loan — which means he will get a bigger credit each month the prime rate stays below his contracted rate.

Rates go down, you win; rates go up, you lose.

And if the borrower isn't happy with the way things are going, he can convert to a fixed rate. But once this is done, that's it — no turning back.

30
Don't Quote Me

There is a new game in town played by the mortgagor and mortgagee. The expert in the game is obviously a graduate of Shaft University (Shaft U for short).

The Shaft U graduate is the borrower in, say, a $60,000 mortgage deed with a 5-year term at 11%. The mortgage is 2 years old.

The mortgagor wants to pay off the mortgage because he is selling and the buyer doesn't want a mortgage, or he came into a financial windfall and doesn't want the debt, or any of a dozen other reasons.

He discovers that the mortgagee is willing to accept a payoff and provide a discharge certificate, but wants six months' interest for the privilege, which could cost the borrower more than three thousand dollars. The mortgage term, having another three years to go, could cost the borrower a lot more, but in this case the lender is being reasonable. But three thousand is three thousand, and the borrower decides that he could make better use of the money than handing it over to the lender.

So the mortgagor starts his game. He does a bit of play acting and lets the lender know that he is sorry, but he can't make the next payment, which of course is a lot of hogwash. The lender is a bit disturbed by this; the borrower merrily goes on ignoring the lender.

Finally, the borrower receives a warning letter from the lender's lawyer, which he promptly tosses in the garbage. Another letter, ditto. And then, *whoopee*, a sheriff's officer arrives at the mortgagor's door and serves him with a writ of foreclosure. Hooray. This is just what the borrower was waiting for!

You see, in the writ the lender can just claim arrears of interest, plus principal, but *not* the six months' penalty he wanted to pay off the mortgage. So the borrower pays off the writ, plus a couple of hundred to the lawyer, and he has just saved himself a bundle.

Well, one can imagine what this sort of behaviour would cost and save if the mortgage were a big one, say a couple of hundred thousand.

However, some lenders are catching on to the game, especially the ones holding the big mortgages, and if they suspect the borrower is playing this little game, they will sue him for the *arrears* owing and *not* for foreclosure. This keeps the affluent borrower on the hook and if he now wants to pay off the mortgage it might cost a bit more than the six months' interest.

If the mortgagor played this game to pay off the mortgage, and there was a junior mortgage registered behind the big one, he would obviously have to move quickly in paying off the writ. The junior mortgagee could march in and bring the arrears of the first mortgage up to date and charge the amount to its mortgage, plus a legal fee, which would put the mortgagor back in square one.

31
Interest Rates

Remember, the more frequent the compounding, the greater the yield to the *lender*. The tables on the following pages will provide helpful information in determining interest calculations for a number of mortgage loans:

1. Interest only loans
2. A fixed principal payment, plus interest
3. A blended payment (interest and principal)

The last column on each page shows the effective annual yield to the lender.

However, before calculating interest, ensure that you are familiar with the Federal Interest Act, and its effect on mortgages. If you cannot obtain a copy locally, write to the Queen's Printer, Ottawa, Ontario, and get one.

Interest only loans

Simply use the rate applicable to the compounding frequency and the period of payment.

Fixed principal payment, plus interest

On the first payment, use the appropriate rate for the entire amount of the loan. On subsequent payments,

use the appropriate rate and apply it to the outstanding principal balance of the loan.

Blended payment (interest and principal)

Calculate the interest using the appropriate rate. The
payment will include interest and principal, so the
balance of the payment will be the amount of principal
to be deducted from the principal balance owing.

For example, a $10,000 loan, 10%, compounded half-
yearly, repayable $100 monthly. The first month's in-
terest will be $81.64 on the $10,000, so the balance of
the payment ($18.36) will be applied to the principal.
Deduct this $18.36 from the $10,000 when estimating
the second payment, so the interest on the second payment will be $9,981,64 × 0.816485, or $81.50. The
balance of this month's payment of $100 will be
$18.50, which will be applied to principal. Repeat this
throughout the loan.

Compounded Monthly

	Payable Monthly	Payable Quarterly	Payable Semi-Annually	Payable Annually
10	0.833333	2.520891	5.105331	10.471307
10¼	0.845167	2.584450	5.235695	10.745514
10½	0.875000	2.648036	5.366192	11.020345
10¾	0.895833	2.711647	5.496825	11.295801
11	0.916667	2.775285	5.627592	11.571884
11¼	0.937500	2.838950	5.758496	11.848594
11½	0.958333	2.902640	5.889533	12.125933
11¾	0.979167	2.966357	6.020706	12.403901
12	1.000000	3.030100	6.152015	12.682503
12¼	1.020833	3.093869	6.283459	12.961736
12½	1.041667	3.157665	6.415039	13.241605
12¾	1.062500	3.221487	6.546754	13.522108
13	1.083333	3.285335	6.678605	13.803248
13¼	1.104167	3.349210	6.810592	14.085026
13½	1.125000	3.413111	6.942715	14.367444
13¾	1.145833	3.477038	7.074975	14.650502
14	1.166667	3.540992	7.207371	14.934203
14¼	1.187500	3.604972	7.339902	15.218546
14½	1.208333	3.668978	7.472571	15.503535
14¾	1.229167	3.733011	7.605375	15.789169
15	1.250000	3.797070	7.738318	16.075452
15¼	1.270833	3.861156	7.871397	16.362382
15½	1.291667	3.925267	8.004612	16.649962
15¾	1.312500	3.989406	8.137965	16.938195
16	1.333333	4.053570	8.271454	17.227078

Compounded Quarterly

	Payable Monthly	Payable Quarterly	Payable Semi-Annually	Payable Annually
10	0.826484	2.500000	5.062500	10.381289
10¼	0.846973	2.562500	5.190664	10.650758
10½	0.867453	2.625000	5.318906	10.920720
10¾	0.887930	2.687500	5.444723	11.191176
11	0.908390	2.750000	5.575625	11.462126
11¼	0.928846	2.812500	5.704102	11.733571
11½	0.949293	2.875000	5.832656	12.005511
11¾	0.969732	2.937500	5.961289	12.277947
12	0.990163	3.000000	6.090000	12.550881
12¼	1.010586	3.062500	6.218789	12.824311
12½	1.031001	3.125000	6.347656	13.098240
12¾	1.051407	3.187500	6.476602	13.372667
13	1.071805	3.250000	6.605625	13.647593
13¼	1.092194	3.312500	6.734727	13.923019
13½	1.112576	3.375000	6.863906	14.198945
13¾	1.132949	3.437500	6.993164	14.475372
14	1.153314	3.500000	7.122500	14.752300
14¼	1.176927	3.562500	7.272628	15.074166
14½	1.194020	3.625000	7.381406	15.307664
14¾	1.214360	3.687500	7.510976	15.586101
15	1.234693	3.750000	7.640625	15.865042
15¼	1.255017	3.812500	7.770351	16.144487
15½	1.275333	3.875000	7.900156	16.424437
15¾	1.295641	3.937500	8.030039	16.704893
16	1.315940	4.000000	8.160000	16.985856

Compounded Half-Yearly

	Payable Monthly	Payable Quarterly	Payable Semi-Annually	Payable Annually
10	0.816485	2.469508	5.000000	10.250000
10¼	0.836478	2.530483	5.125000	10.512656
10½	0.856452	2.591423	5.250000	10.775625
10¾	0.876405	2.652326	5.375000	11.038906
11	0.896338	2.713193	5.500000	11.302500
11¼	0.916254	2.774024	5.625000	11.566406
11½	0.936149	2.834819	5.750000	11.830625
11¾	0.956024	2.895578	5.875000	12.095156
12	0.975879	2.956301	6.000000	12.360000
12¼	0.995715	3.016989	6.125000	12.625156
12½	1.015532	3.077641	6.250000	12.890625
12¾	1.035329	3.138257	6.375000	13.156406
13	1.055107	3.198837	6.500000	13.422500
13¼	1.074866	3.259382	6.625000	13.688906
13½	1.094605	3.319892	6.750000	13.955625
13¾	1.114325	3.380366	6.875000	14.222656
14	1.134026	3.440804	7.000000	14.490000
14¼	1.153708	3.501208	7.125000	14.757656
14½	1.173370	3.561576	7.250000	15.025625
14¾	1.193013	3.621909	7.375000	15.293906
15	1.212679	3.682207	7.500000	15.562500
15¼	1.232243	3.742470	7.625000	15.831406
15½	1.251830	3.802697	7.750000	16.100625
15¾	1.271397	3.862890	7.875000	16.370156
16	1.290946	3.923048	8.000000	16.640000

Compounded Annually

	Payable Monthly	Payable Quarterly	Payable Semi-Annually	Payable Annually
10	0.797414	2.411369	4.880885	10.000000
10¼	0.816485	2.469508	5.000000	10.250000
10½	0.835516	2.527548	5.118980	10.500000
10¾	0.854507	2.585489	5.237826	10.750000
11	0.873459	2.643333	5.356538	11.000000
11¼	0.892372	2.701079	5.475115	11.250000
11½	0.911247	2.758727	5.593560	11.500000
11¾	0.930082	2.816279	5.711873	11.750000
12	0.948879	2.873734	5.830052	12.000000
12¼	0.967638	2.931094	5.948101	12.250000
12½	0.986358	2.988357	6.066017	12.500000
12¾	1.005040	3.045525	6.183803	12.750000
13	1.023684	3.102598	6.301458	13.000000
13¼	1.042291	3.159577	6.418983	13.250000
13½	1.060860	3.216461	6.536379	13.500000
13¾	1.079391	3.273252	6.653645	13.750000
14	1.097885	3.329948	6.770783	14.000000
14¼	1.116342	3.386552	6.887792	14.250000
14½	1.134762	3.443063	7.004673	14.500000
14¾	1.153145	3.499481	7.121426	14.750000
15	1.171492	3.555808	7.238053	15.000000
15¼	1.189801	3.612042	7.354553	15.250000
15½	1.208075	3.668185	7.470926	15.500000
15¾	1.226313	3.724237	7.587174	15.750000
16	1.244514	3.780199	7.703296	16.000000

32
Deductible Mortgage Interest

Aside from deducting mortgage interest on investment properties, how about deducting the interest on
the mortgage you have on your own home, your principal dwelling? In the United States it is easy. Just do
it, because that's the way it is for the lucky American
homeowner. And what a difference it makes in the income tax one pays.

Take a U.S.A. mortgage of 9% for example. When
one knocks the interest off the annual tax bite, it is no
longer 9%. Here is what it *really* is.

Tax Bracket	Real Mortgage Rate
25%	6.75%
30%	6.30%
35%	5.85%
40%	5.40%
50%	4.50%

That's right. If one is in a 40% tax bracket in the
USA, the house mortgage today will cost less than 6%.

We pay our mortgage interest in after-tax dollars.
Here is what we really pay on a 10½% mortgage using
the same formula:

Tax Bracket	Comparable Rate
25%	14.00%
30%	15.00%
35%	16.15%
40%	17.50%
50%	21.00%

What this means is that, for example, the Canadian borrower in the 40% tax bracket would be paying 17½% interest on his mortgage if he had the privilege of deducting it from his income tax, to bring it down to the 10½% after deduction.

We pay 10½% now after taxes, and the comparable American pays 5.4% *just about half*. If our 40% bracket borrower could deduct that 10½% from tax, the rate would be 6.3%. Still higher than the American.

However gloomy the foregoing, there is one way to deduct the interest paid on your principal dwelling mortgage. Our Income Tax Act allows one's principal dwelling to be used as security to obtain a loan for the purpose of acquiring investments that will produce income. Of course you can really use anything for security that a lender will accept to get the money, but many of us overlook the good old homestead.

This doesn't mean that you can suddenly purchase an interest-bearing security with your spare cash and then start deducting the interest on your mortgage. The money must be specifically borrowed for a specific investment purpose, which means that you would take out a new mortgage on your home, and invest the entire proceeds in the investment venture. You will have to prove this to the income tax people. Then you may deduct the mortgage interest from your income tax.

There are variations, of course. If one borrowed

$40,000 by a mortgage and only used $30,000 of it for investment, then only the interest on the $30,000 portion could be deducted, and not the interest on the entire loan. Again, you will have to prove it.

However, before you rush out and borrow a pile for investment purposes, examine it. There would be no point in borrowing money at 10½% and lending it at 9%. That would obviously be a losing proposition, so you must ensure that your investment will show a profit over the net costs of borrowing the money, regardless of its nature.

Also, check with your bank manager regarding the latest rules about Registered Retirement Savings Plans. You may be in for a pleasant surprise in the way you may engineer an interest-deductible loan using your home as security, for investing in your RRSP.

33
Caveat for Mortgage Lenders

An elderly couple asked me for some advice on where they should invest about $60,000 in second mortgages.

I asked why they wanted second mortgages, and the response was that in addition to receiving a higher rate of interest, they won't bother to pay income tax on the interest.

When I pointed out that, regardless of where earned income comes from, it must be reported, they replied: "Everybody does it."

This sort of thinking can get one in a mess of trouble. Agents from the income tax department make a practice of periodically surveying registry offices to identify private mortgage loans. And the reason is very basic.

When one receives interest income from conventional borrowers like banks and trust companies, the one paying the interest provides the lender with T5 information slips. One copy is sent to the government, and two to the lender. The lender knows the government is aware of the money received, so naturally includes the information when preparing the annual income tax return.

But borrowers of private mortgage funds by the

thousands never bother to fill out these forms and pass a copy along to the government. They don't do it basically because it is of no benefit to them; they are the borrowers in household mortgages and the interest is not deductible in any way. They are just glad to be able to pay the interest and couldn't care less what the lender does about income tax.

If the government allowed such borrowers a small deduction on their income taxes, say 2½% of such payments, provided they filled out and mailed the T5 slips, the government's income would dramatically increase.

On a $20,000 mortgage at 12%, the interest paid annually would be about $2,400. Allow the borrower to deduct $60 from income tax and you can be sure that T5 slip will go in the mail. The lender would then realize he or she is hooked, and will cough up.

Well, what happens to lenders who don't receive the T5 slips and don't bother to report the income? If one has been getting away with it for years, the mortgage itself might have to be sold to settle everything when caught. Or even the old homestead. Phew!

First of all, tax returns for the years involved are reassessed. Then, in most cases, a penalty is charged equal to 25% of the additional tax assessed. On top of this will be interest on the assessed tax; and the total of tax, penalty and interest can be quite substantial.

Where significant amounts of mortgage interest income have not been reported, the taxpayer's affairs will be investigated and one may end up being prosecuted for tax evasion. That can mean criminal fines and jail sentences.

Conviction can be humiliating

Conviction means details of one's sticky fingers

reported in the press. How would you like to have your friends and neighbors read about something like that? And what about the cruel taunts thrown at your kids in school?

However, do not despair. There is a voluntary disclosure policy available which enables taxpayers to report hidden income without the headaches of prosecution. It won't mean freedom from financial penalties, but it will mean a good night's sleep.

This voluntary disclosure will be subjected to verification, and if it is shown that the taxpayer disclosed only those amounts which one thought the government would become aware of, it will not be considered as voluntary, but rather as an attempt to further deceive the government.

And here's a horrible thought: When one expires, the government takes a good look at all the assets in the estate. When it comes across mortgages, it will naturally want to see some evidence of tax payments made on the income.

Sooner or later, the government is going to get it.

34
Real Property Definitions

Abstract A written, condensed history of title to a parcel or real property, recorded in a land registry office.

Abuttals The bounding of a parcel of land by other land, street, river, etc. A boundary.

Acceleration Clause On mortgage payment default, the entire balance of the loan is due and immediately payable.

Administrator One who has charge of the estate of a deceased person who died without a will, or one who did not appoint an executor. Appointed by court order.

Adverse Possession When someone, other than the owner, takes physical possession of property, without the owner's consent.

Agent One who legally represents an individual or corporate body.

Agreement of Sale Written agreement whereby one agrees to buy, and another agrees to sell, according to the terms and conditions in the agreement.

Agreement to Lease	Written agreement whereby one agrees to lease real property to another, according to the terms of the agreement.
Amortization	To extinguish a loan by means of a sinking fund.
Appraisal	A written estimate of the market value of real property, made by a qualified expert.
Appreciation	Increased market value of real property.
Appurtenances	Additional rights that are an adjunction to real property.
Assessed Value	Value of real property set by a municipality for taxation purposes.
Assessor	Person employed by a municipality or other government body empowered to place valuation on property for taxation purposes.
Assignment	Legal transfer of interest in real property or a mortgage from one person to another.
Assumption Agreement	An agreement whereby a person other than the mortgagor convenants to perform the obligations in the mortgage deed.
Attornment of Rent	Taking of rents by mortgagee in possession to protect his rights in case of default by mortgagor.
Bond	A binding agreement to stengthen the covenant of performance.
Broker	A person who legally trades in real estate for another, for compensation.

Certificate of Charge Provincial government acknowledgement of registration of mortgage in a land titles office.

Certificate of Title Provincial government acknowledgement of registration of title deed in a land titles office.

Chattels Movable possessions, such as furniture, personal possessions, etc. A furnace, before it is installed, is a movable possession. Once installed, it is not.

Chattel Mortgage A mortgage on movable possessions, personal property.

Closing The time at which a real estate transaction is concluded legally in a registry office.

Cloud on Title An impairment to title of real property such as executed judgement, mortgage, lien, etc., registered legally against the property.

CMHC Canada Mortgage and Housing Corporation, a Crown agency administering Canada's National Housing Act.

Commission Financial remuneration paid to an agent for selling or leasing property, based on an agreed percentage of the amount involved.

Consideration Something of value for compensation.

Contract An agreement upon lawful consideration which binds the parties to a performance.

Conveyance	Transmitting title of real property from one to another.
Covenant	Solemn agreement.
Covenantee	Lender in a (mortgage) deed.
Covenantor	Borrower in a (mortgage) deed.
Date of Maturity	In mortgages, the last day of the term of the mortgage.
Deed	A document containing an agreement that has been signed, sealed, and containing proof of its delivery; effective only on the date of delivery. (Mortgage deed, title deed, etc.)
Demise	To transfer or convey an estate for a term of years, or life.
Deposit	Money or other consideration of value given as pledge for fulfillment of a contract or agreement.
Depreciation	Reduction in market value of property. Also used to indicate capital cost allowance.
Dower	Rights of wife or widow in freehold property owned by her husband.
Easement	A right acquired to use another's land or buildings, generally for access to some other adjoining property.
Encroachment	Undue or unlawful trespass on another's property, usually caused by a building, or part of a building, or obstruction.
Encumbrance	Any legal claim registered against property.

Equity The financial interest of a property owner in excess of any encumbrances, limited by its market value.

Escheat Conveyance of property to the Crown (government) due to intestate person dying or leaving no heirs.

Escrow A deed or contract delivered to a third party to be held until the payment or fulfillment of the agreement.

Estate One's interest in lands and any other subject of property.

Exclusive Listing An agreement granting sole and exclusive rights to an agent.

Executor Person legally appointed by testator to carry out the terms of his will.

Fee Simple Absolute ownership of property.

Fee Tail Property ownership, limited to some particular heirs.

Fixture Permanent improvements to property that remain with it.

Foreclosure A legally enforced transfer of real property ordered by a court to satisfy unpaid debts. The most common is a foreclosure by a mortgagee.

Freehold Property held in fee simple (untrammelled tenure) or fee tail (for the term of the owner's life).

Frontage Property line facing street.

Gale Date The date on which interest is charged.

Grant	An instrument of conveyance transferring property from one to another.
Grantee	Person to whom a conveyance is made; one who receives legal transfer of property from another; the buyer.
Grantor	Person who makes a conveyance; one who transfers property to another; the seller.
Hereditament	Property that may be inherited.
Hypothec	Lien on real estate (Quebec).
Hypothecary Creditor	Mortgagee (Quebec).
Hypothecary Debtor	Mortgagor (Quebec).
Indenture	An agreement between two or more parties. Originally, indentures were duplicates placed together and cut in a wavy line, so that the two papers could be identified as being authentic by corresponding to each other.
Instrument	A writing instructing one in regard to something that has been agreed upon.
Intestate	Not having a will.
Joint Tenancy	Ownership of real property by two or more persons; when one dies, his share automatically passes to the survivor(s).
Judgement	Binding decision of the court.
Landed Property	Having an interest in and pertaining to land.

Landlord   A lessor. One who allows another to occupy his land or building for a consideration.

Lease   Binding contract between a landlord (lessor) and tenant (lessee) for the occupation of premises or land for a specified period of time for financial or other consideration.

Leasehold   Property held by lease.

Leaseholder   Tenant under a lease.

Lessee   The tenant. One who pays rent.

Lessor   The person granting use of property to another.

Lien   A legal claim affecting property.

Lis pendens   Notice of commencement of court action, recorded against title of property.

Market Value   The courts have defined this as being the highest price estimated in terms of money which a property will bring, if exposed for sale in the open market, allowing a reasonable time to find a purchaser who buys with knowledge of all the uses to which it may be put, and for which it is capable of being used.

Mechanic's Lien   A lien filed and registered against property by a person or corporate body, for labour and/or materials supplied for the improvement of the property.

Moratorium   Provincial statute deferment of mortgage principal payments during depression. Non-existent now.

Mortgage	What this book is all about.
Mortgage Bonds	Bond holders are represented by a trustee, who is the mortgagee. Bonds can be traded, making them more flexible than individual mortgages.
Mortgaged Out	Situation whereby total mortgage debt on property equals or exceeds market value of property.
Mortgagee	The lender in a mortgage deed. The one receiving the mortgage.
Mortgagor	The borrower in a mortgage deed. The one giving the mortgage.
NHA	National Housing Act.
Option	An agreement whereby one has the exclusive right to purchase another's property at a specified price, with a time limit.
Personalty	Personal property, chattels.
Postponement Clause	In mortgaging, the agreement of an equitable mortgagee to allow the mortgagor to renew or replace a senior mortgage that becomes due before such equitable mortgage.
Power of Attorney	Legal authority for one to act on behalf of another.
Prepayment Clause	In a mortgage, an agreement giving the mortgagor the privilege of paying additional sums off the principal balance over and above the agreed payments.
Principal	A person or corporate body employing an agent.

Principal Balance In a mortgage, the outstanding dollar amount owing on the debt.

Quit Claim Deed A full release of one's interest in property to another, usually executed between mortgagees and mortgagors.

Real Estate Landed property (land).

Real Property Land *and* buildings thereon, and rights thereof.

Realtor Certification mark being the property of the Canadian Real Estate Association. Designates broker-member of Association.

Realty Real property.

Rest The date upon which the amount between the parties to a mortgage is altered. It is not necessarily the date upon which payment is made, unless so agreed in the mortgage deed.

Sales Agreement Purchase of property without obtaining title deed until a specified further sum of money is paid to the vendor.

Socage A tenure of land held by the tenant in performance of specified services or by payment of rent, and not requiring military service (history).

Straight Loan In mortgaging, a mortgage with no principaly payments. Interest only.

Survey Surveyor's report of mathematical boundaries of land, showing location of buildings, physical features, and quantity of land.

Tenancy in Common	Ownership of real property by two or more persons, whereby on the death of one, his share is credited to his own estate.
Tenant	The one who pays rent for the right to occupy land or buildings.
Tenant in Tail	Holder of an estate limited to the heirs of his body. The line of heirs is called entail.
Tenement	Property held by tenant.
Tenure	The right of holding property.
Title Deed	Proof of legal ownership of property.
Title Search	Research of records in registry or land titles office to determine history and chain of ownership of property.
Usury	An unconscionable and exorbitant rate of interest.
Zoning	Specified limitation on the use of land, the construction and use of buildings, in a defined section of a municipality.

The Last Word

Remember, when agreeing to give a second mortgage (or third) to a vendor as part of the purchase price in buying real estate, insert a clause in the agreement whereby you, as the mortgagor, are to have the right of first refusal in the event that the mortgage is to be sold.

If it is sold, it will most likely be sold at a discount, and in the event that you are financially flush, you could save some money. Right?

It appears to be an actuarial fact that over a period of any twenty years, sixteen mortgagors in one hundred will not live to complete the mortgage payments. The homeowner naturally would like to ensure that if the breadwinner is gone, his family will be left with a debt-free roof over its head.

Life insurance companies are ready to oblige by providing term insurance (the cheapest life insurance one can buy) to cover the outstanding dollar balance owing on the mortgages. As the principal balance owing is reduced, the insurance coverage is reduced, the object being to have them both go down to a nil balance together.

Think about it, and do your best to fit it into your budget.

The closing advice I gave in my book *Canadian Real Estate* is what I am going to repeat here, because I believe it.

Every book has an ending, but not this one. This book can be just the beginning for you and the future financial security of you and your loved ones.

The older you get, the more you will appreciate the fact that true friends are few and far between and, therefore, you have to learn to look after your financial interests without leaning on, or crawling to, someone else for help.

If you are young, you are doubly fortunate. The opportunites for your future security are simply waiting for you to embrace them, and they could very well be in real estate. The basic rules of real estate success are (1) know the ground rules, (2) act wisely but not hastily, and (3) don't be greedy.

Get involved. Don't dream. Don't procrastinate. Get a piece of the action — even a little piece. And to the approximately 50,000 real estate agents in Canada who spend most of their time creating financial real estate success for others, while living on the promise of commissions, I have this piece of advice: If *you* want to make it over the long haul, you'll very seldom do it on your commissions. You *must* get involved.

The foregoing was the final word of advice in *Canadian Real Estate*, but I want to add something else to it, with the sincere hope that many of you, especially the young, will follow this advice. As we all know, the federal government has provided a very generous pension plan that is tied to the cost of living. It must surely be the world's greatest pension.

Well, in the likely event that you will not retire on a federal government pension, what are you doing about your old age? The young generally don't like to think about thirty or so years ahead, it's just too far off. But with good health it will come just as surely as death and taxes.

Here is my suggestion. Go into the country, find a nice piece of concession-corner land you can buy with about $3,000 down, mortgage the balance for what you can carry without hurting yourself too much (which will dictate the purchase price) and then, forget it until you are fifty-five or so. Sell it and live off the interest. That's your assured pension.

Don't think for one minute that land in this world is going to get cheaper. It won't. Not because I say so, but because, as the late Will Rogers reminds us, "Buy land, they're not making any more of it."

If you follow this advice, and a couple of years later someone offers you double your equity, *don't sell*. Resist the temptation to take the profit and buy that new car or take that vacation. This is *your pension* that buyer is tampering with!

Go on, get a piece of land. Enjoy it. Grow some vegetables on your pension. Rent it to a farmer. Stand on it and look around, you're a land owner!

Hang onto your pension.

The foregoing piece of advice may not go down too well with some economists, but what I am attempting to do here is encourage you to take some of that money you will be pouring down your drains of frivolity and bury it in land.

In 1942 the author was a Flight Sergeant stationed at an air observers school in Malton, Ontario. That same year, a young man (not me, unfortunately) purchased 97 acres of land near the air station for $12,000 with $2,000 down. I had access to $2,000 at the time, but buying a parcel of land was the furthest thing from my mind. There were too many weekends in Detroit to take care of!

Well, that same man sold this land about 25 years later for $1,300,000.

The next time you get some urge to go flying off on some expensive holiday, or feel the need of an expensive piece of tin on wheels, forget it. Just once, forget it, and buy a piece of land. Believe me, you will not regret it.

And a mortgage can make it possible.